never burn out

DISCOVER THE REALITY OF YOUR IDENTITY

Daniel H. Park

Copyright © 2011 by Daniel Park

All rights reserved. This book is protected under the copyright laws of the United States of America. This book may not be copied or reprinted for commercial gain or profit. The use of short quotations or occasional page copying for personal or group study is permitted and encouraged.

Scripture quotations marked (NKJV) are taken from the NEW KING JAMES VERSION. Copyright © 1982 by Thomas Nelson, Inc. Used by permission. All rights reserved. Scripture quotations marked (ESV) are from THE HOLY BIBLE, ENGLISH STANDARD VERSION® (ESV®), Copyright © 2001 by Crossway, a publishing ministry of Good News Publishers. Used by permission. All rights reserved. Scripture quotations marked (NIV) are from THE HOLY BIBLE, NEW INTERNATIONAL VERSION®, NIV® Copyright © 1973, 1978, 1984, 2011 by Biblica, Inc.™ Used by permission. All rights reserved worldwide. Scripture quotations marked (NASB) taken from the NEW AMERICAN STANDARD BIBLE®, Copyright © 1960, 1962, 1963, 1968, 1971, 1972, 1973, 1975, 1977, 1995 by The Lockman Foundation. Used by permission. - Scripture quotations marked (NLT) are taken from THE HOLY BIBLE, NEW LIVING TRANSLATION, Copyright © 1996, 2004, 2007 by Tyndale House Foundation. Used by permission of Tyndale House Publishers, Inc., Carol Stream, Illinois 60188. All rights reserved. Scripture quotations marked (GW) taken from GOD'S WORD®, © 1995 God's Word to the Nations. Used by permission of Baker Publishing Group. Scripture taken from THE MESSAGE, Copyright © 1993, 1994, 1995, 1996, 2000, 2001, 2002. Used by permission of NavPress Publishing Group. Scripture quotations taken from the AMPLIFIED® BIBLE, Copyright © 1954, 1958, 1962, 1964, 1965, 1987 by The Lockman Foundation. Used by permission. Scripture quotations marked (ISV) taken from THE HOLY BIBLE: INTERNATIONAL STANDARD VERSION®, Copyright © 1996-2008 by The ISV Foundation. ALL RIGHTS RESERVED INTERNATIONALLY. Used by permission. The Holy Bible King James Version: 1611 Edition. Public domain. - Webster Bible Translation: Public Domain. - Weymouth Translation: The New Testament in Modern Speech (New York: Harper and Row Publishers, Inc., 1903.) Public domain.

Published by XP Publishing
P.O. Box 1017
Maricopa, Arizona 85139
United States of America

ISBN 978-1-936101-54-2

www.XPPublishing.com

David,

May you be a VOICE to God's KEY LEADERS! You are carrying the WORD in SEASON

never Burn out

Endorsements

This book is a "Must Read" for every believer who wants to experience the thrill of discovering their true identity in the Person of Jesus Christ. As you read this powerful, life-changing book, you will find yourself exchanging your old negative self-image into a New Creation Image. The frustrations of trying to please God through self-performance that has led so many believers and ministers into experiencing "Burn-Out" will be a thing of the past. It is a revelation of righteousness that will free the reader from the negative self-images of guilt and condemnation. This is the most comprehensive book I have ever read on this subject. It is masterfully written using practical, easy to understand illustrations that effectively communicate powerful truths that will bring a new and higher level of freedom to the life of the reader. The revelations found in the pages of this book will launch you into a thrilling, fulfilling, joyful life of never-ending revival. This book is like an exhilarating breath of fresh-air that you will want to read over and over and share and recommend to all of your friends.

Dr. A.L. Gill,
International Author/Speaker/Bible Teacher
www.Gill Ministries.com

NEVER BURN OUT: Discover the Reality of your Identity

Burn Out is not an uncommon condition in this hour. Why do many burn out? Daniel Park vulnerably shares from his own experiences and insights he has learned. Not only will this book give you keys to protect you or heal you from burn out, it will also ground you in your God-given identity in Christ. The revelation of your identity in Christ will keep you in peace in all you do. This is a wonderful book. I LIKE IT!

Patricia King,
Television Host, Author/Speaker
www.xpmedia.com

In this generation, God is raising up powerful leaders who will equip the body of Christ through fresh revelatory teaching. Daniel is one of these powerful leaders who carry the spirit of wisdom and revelation. Daniel is a young man who God is raising up to carry the message of revival and His Kingdom's power. We have known Daniel personally for over 7 years now and have experienced his powerful teaching that sets people on fire for God. Daniel teaches people how to be the walking revival and live in an ever-increasing revival each day. Daniel's book is full of refreshing insight and practical steps to experience revival and sustain it. By reading this book, not only will you experience revival, but you will also be able to teach others to experience revival. As Daniel devoted much time to carefully study the Word with precision, there is powerful revelation that is unleashed in this book. We pray that everyone will not only read this book but meditate upon the truths set forth in it so that radical transformation will take place in everyone's life.

Ryan & Joanne Lee,
Lead Pastors, Blessed International Fellowship

NEVER BURN OUT: Discover the Reality of your Identity

Daniel Park is truly a revivalist at heart, and seeing that you can only convey to others what you carry on the inside, this book has dynamite power. I love his practical, picturesque language as he paints parables which cause your eyes to be opened and inspires you to desire the same passionate heart to be a carrier of revival. You will discover your true identity in Christ that will bring you in the liberty and power of the Spirit to take the Kingdom by force, carrying and releasing the glory of God everywhere you go!

Elsabe Briers,
Itinerant Minister, Agape Life Ministries
www.agapelifeministriesinc.com

While some books are written to be relevant to a certain age group, this book is for those of all ages and stages of life. Daniel addresses areas of confrontation that every age segment of readers must deal with.

The issues that Daniel deals with in this book are pivotal areas that need to resolved if we are going to reach our potential.

One key word that Daniel emphasizes is "FOCUS". We must focus on the promises of God, rather than the problems that bombard us. This book will help you to do just that.

Although this author is young, he communicates a message of spiritual depth and maturity. His dedication to prayer and evangelism takes him to many parts of the world, reaching this generation.

Dr. Ralph Wilkerson,
Evangelist and Founding Pastor of
Melodyland Christian Center.

NEVER BURN OUT: Discover the Reality of your Identity

Daniel Park has written an uplifting and life-affirming guide to the promises of God's love. For anyone who is feeling lost or stagnant in their faith, *Never Burn Out* will show you the freedom of knowing your true identity in Jesus. By clearing some misconceptions about the body of Christ, you will see that such things as shame and competition are not the will of God, and that we are meant to experience revival all around us. Daniel Park is an exciting young leader who is inspiring believers to tap into the potential of their relationship with God. I would highly recommend *Never Burn Out* to believers young and old who are looking for a breath of life in their faith.

Matthew Barnett,
Co-founder of the Dream Center,
Senior Pastor, Angelus Temple,
Best-Selling Author
www.dreamcenter.org

Daniel communicates in an easy to read – easy to understand style. His subject is vital. I can't imagine anyone reading his book and not finding some fresh thoughts to help them in their walk with God.

Bayless Conley,
Senior Pastor, Cottonwood Church
www.cottonwood.org

Acknowledgments

- Thank you Holy Spirit. I'd be so stupid and lost without You.

- Thanks to my wife for being simply the greatest.

- Thank you Jim Wies, Carol Martinez, and the rest of the XP Publishing team for your first-class help.

- Thank you to those who read the manuscript and contributed with valuable input: Papa Gill, Janet Jun, Roberta Foran, Cheryl Chew, and Tom Hartman

- Thank you to those who endorsed the book; way before writing an endorsement, you have all made such a difference in my life.

TABLE OF CONTENTS

Preface 13
1. Living in Ever-Increasing Revival 17
2. Know Your True Identity 31
3. You Are a New Creation 47
4. You Are Righteous 57
5. You Are Holy 69
6. You Have Dominion 93
7. You Are in Covenant with God 117
8. You Are a Walking Revival 133
9. You Are Adopted 151
10. You Are His Bride 169
11. Honor Your Birthright 185
Addendum: How to Kill a Revival 193

Preface

This book was written to help you never burn out

Have you ever met a burnt out Christian? Do you know anybody who used to be so excited about the Lord, but isn't now?

One of the biggest reasons Christians burn out is that although they know what they should and shouldn't do, they do not really know who they are.

There is nothing more tiring than trying to be someone you don't believe you are. For me as a man, trying to act like a woman for an entire day would be the most exhausting day of my life!

This book is not calling you to try to be somebody you aren't, but is encouraging you to be who you really are.

Historically, many revivals have burned up and burnt out. But this book was written with a vision to see the Church and each believer living in ever-increasing revival; only increasing in their passion for God, and in their experience of His presence and power.

This book was written to help you experience the God of grace

Many of the thoughts we have about ourselves are in total opposition to God's thoughts about us. As you read, your false self-portraits will be burned up in the fire of God's grace.

NEVER BURN OUT: Discover the Reality of your Identity

"Grace and truth came through Jesus Christ." (John 1:16 ESV)

Through Jesus Christ, we have received an abundance of grace from God. But amazingly, God's grace doesn't just reveal the truth about God, but also the truth about ourselves.

While this book will educate you about yourself, and you will definitely be encouraged and empowered to live with greater confidence, this book is ultimately about Who God is. He takes center-stage.

It may appear, from the chapter titles in the table of contents, that most of the chapters pertain to who you are. But it is my hope that this book will ultimately leave you in total awe and worship of the God Who has made you into a new creation (Ch. 3), Who is your righteousness (Ch. 4), Who is your holiness (Ch. 5), Who has restored your dominion (Ch. 6), Who is your covenant partner (Ch. 7), Who is your glorious revival (Ch. 8), Who is your adoptive Father (Ch. 9), and Who is your passionate Bridegroom (Ch. 10).

This book was written to help you receive more from God

God is the perfect quarterback who has sent His blessings our way, but quite often we are in handcuffs, unable to receive. Do you feel that describes your life?

Quite often, the blockage doesn't have to do with God's unwillingness, but rather our uneducated minds and unbelieving hearts.

"And you will know the truth, and the truth will set you free." (John 8:32)

Preface

This book will educate you in the truth about who you are. You will clearly discover the reality of your identity! And as you do, this book will serve as a key to unlock your hands of faith, so you can receive everything God desires for you to have.

As you are freed up to receive more from God, you will be in position to give more to this lost and dying world.

When I initially began to receive the insights and understanding I am sharing in this book, I started receiving more wisdom, refreshing, and empowerment in just five minutes of prayer, than I used to get in five hours of prayer. I also began to see the river of God flow out of me with less blockage and more power. I expect the same thing to happen to you.

"Freely you received, freely give." (Matthew 10:8 NASB)

This book was written to help you become a revivalist

What the world needs is not just persuasive words of human wisdom, but an undeniable encounter with their Creator who loves them. This is called revival.

Revival will be a theme throughout this book. Revival is what bored, burnt out Christians need. Revival is what dead churches need. Revival is what our desperate world needs. It's my dream that our churches will become revival centers, and that every Christian will become overflowing carriers of the presence of God; that it will no longer be the common condition for so many church attendees not to have experienced the indescribable presence of the Lord.

Therefore, this book was written to train you to be a revivalist; someone who will be a true carrier and channel of the revival fire of the Holy Spirit.

NEVER BURN OUT: Discover the Reality of your Identity

This book was written to empower your faith

The intention of this book is not just to elevate your hopes, but to ignite your faith. Hope is based on what will happen in the future "one day." Faith is based on what has already happened in the past; on what God has already declared!

This book is going to present to you what has already taken place and what God has already declared over your life. Each chapter will clearly present to you what God has already done for you. You will see who you are in Christ by grace and through the cross! The truths in this book are not future hopes, but present realities that you need to believe, experience, and enjoy.

> What is faith? Faith is my acceptance of God's fact. It always has its foundations in the past. This is faith – to believe that you have already got it. Only that which relates to the past is faith in this sense. Those who say, "God can" or "God may" or "God must" or "God will" do not necessarily believe at all. Faith always says, "God has done it."[1] – Watchman Nee

I'm not saying that hope is not a precious jewel, but according to the Bible, hope doesn't move mountains – faith does. Hope is not what absolutely pleases God – faith is. Hope alone doesn't bring answered prayers – faith does! Mere hope doesn't launch us into being a revivalist, walking by faith does!

It's my prayer that this book will be used by the Holy Spirit to prevent you from experiencing burn out; and heal you from being burned out. I pray that it will give you the keys you need so that, instead of burning out, you will only go from glory to glory! That is God's will for your life.

---

[1] Watchman Nee, *Normal Christian Life*, pp. 68-69

Chapter 1

Living in Ever-Increasing Revival

The opposite of burnout is revival. You are either burning out, or living in ever-increasing revival.

The focus of this book is not so much "how to dodge a burn out" as it is "how to live in ever-increasing revival." We are on the winning offensive end, not the helpless defensive end.

This chapter will show you what revival looks like, and why you should expect nothing other than ever-increasing revival for your life.

What is revival? Revival is the invasion of the glory of God upon the earth. In revival, people actively experience the glory of God.

What is the glory of God? It is the tangible, experiential, undeniable, manifest presence of God.

NEVER BURN OUT: Discover the Reality of your Identity

Those who experience the glory of God will find it difficult to ever again doubt the reality of God. When I experienced the glory of God fourteen years ago, I found it utterly impossible to question the reality of God – because it was more real than anything!

The glory is the oxygen of heaven, and we do not have to die to get to breathe it in. You can experience the glory of God now. That is revival. Any so-called "revival" without the glory of God is only religious hype, because revival is the manifestation of the glory of God.

Allow me to paint a big mural that will present to you what revival is all about.

In Revival, You Experience Heavenly Joy and Pleasure

The Psalmist wrote, "... In Your presence is fullness of joy; In Your right hand there are pleasures forever" (Psalm 16:11 NASB).

In 1727, revival broke out among a small group of believers in Germany, who called themselves the Moravians. They were celebrating communion, when the glory of God came powerfully upon them. When I say the glory of God came upon them, I'm not talking about a strange force or a mystical power, I'm actually talking about a person: the Holy Spirit.

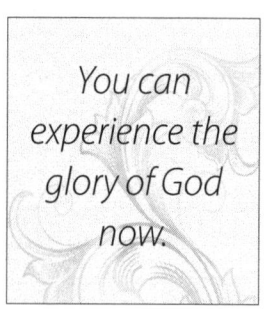
You can experience the glory of God now.

The Holy Spirit is the "Spirit of glory."[2] He is Mr. Revival. As water is wet, the Holy Spirit is revival.

---
[2] 1 Peter 4:14

Living in Ever-Increasing Revival

When the Moravians were absolutely filled with Mr. Revival, they turned to one another and asked, "Wait, did I die?"[3] They were experiencing so much supernatural joy, they thought they had died and gone to heaven.

This revival lasted for one hundred years.

Have you heard of Jonathan Edwards, the famous preacher from the First Great Awakening (1730s-1750s)? He documented that during the revival that shook early America, "some who are the subjects of it [the revival] have been in a kind of ecstasy, wherein they have been carried beyond themselves..."[4]

Young people who are turning to sexual escapades, alcohol, the occult, or psychedelic drugs to have ecstatic experiences are settling for Satan's cheap imitation of the glory of God.

In the 1970s, a revival swept this nation that became known as the Jesus Movement. Many hippies were born-again and became known as the "Jesus People". One article read, "according to a survey of [the] Jesus People, 91% had premarital sex, 85% drank alcohol, 67% smoked, and 90% used drugs before conversion; after conversion, this percentage dropped down to nearly zero."[5]

When they had tasted the real glory of God, they threw out the cheap imitation.

In Revival, the Word Gets Out

Historically, the news of revival spreads like wildfire; usually by word of mouth, not fancy advertisement or self-promotion.

---
[3] A.W. Tozer, *When He Is Come*
[4] Thomas S. Kidd, *The Great Awakening*, p. 119
[5] Association of Young Journalists and Writers: http://www.ayjw.org/print_articles.php?id=620478&title=Getting%20High%20on%20Jesus:%20The%20Jesus%20Movement

NEVER BURN OUT: Discover the Reality of your Identity

When you are in revival, people will start hearing about your dynamic relationship with God, and you will not need to promote yourself.

John Wesley, a man who walked in revival, said that when you are on fire, people will come to watch you burn.

Millenniums before radio, television, and the internet, Paul and Silas were known around the world as the ones who "turned the world upside down."[6]

In revival, it's not uncommon for large crowds to gather. Jesus and Paul seemingly attracted crowds wherever they went.

When you are in revival, it doesn't matter whether you are an introvert or extrovert, whether you are extremely talented or not; your impact upon lives will be beyond what you could've ever asked for or imagined.

> "Now all glory to God, who is able, through his mighty power at work within us, to accomplish infinitely more than we might ask or think" (Ephesians 3:20 NLT).

Revival Is Marked by Many Souls Coming into the Kingdom

When you are in revival, people who come in contact with you will want to be saved and go to heaven, because they can feel heaven's atmosphere all around you.

When I experienced the glory of God, I became a firm believer in heaven, because I knew, "there must be more where that came from!"

Our church was out on the streets of Santa Ana doing an outreach, and one man kept telling us that he was feeling this powerful energy around us. So, I extended my hand and asked

[6] See Acts 17:6

Living in Ever-Increasing Revival

him to shake it, because I knew that he would feel a stronger measure of this energy. As he shook my hand, he was taken aback, saying, "Wow, I really feel it!" This man showed up at our church the next day, because he was so drawn to "the energy" – which is really the glory of God.

Once, Charles Finney – a key figure in the Second Great Awakening (early 1800s) – walked into a large factory, minding his own business. As he began checking out the machinery, the factory workers began to break down one by one and started weeping uncontrollably [like little babies] over their sins.[7] Since they weren't able to continue their work, Finney took some time to lead them to Christ, and revival broke out in that factory, as sinners came to repentance!

I love how the jailer begged Paul and Silas, "What must I do to be saved?"[8] When it's not the preacher begging, but the people begging to know the God you represent – that is a sign of revival.

Revivals Bring Social Reforms

Revival is like a bomb. A bomb detonates from the inside out. Revival first explodes in the heart, then it goes out into world and brings social transformation.

The Cane Ridge revival, which broke out in Kentucky, rallied up Christians against slavery and for women's rights.[9] The revived Christians became the strongest advocates and pioneers for freedom and equality, and they succeeded in their endeavor.

The Salvation Army, which is one of the world's largest distributers of humanitarian aid, was born in revival that was

---
[7] The Gospel Truth: http://www.gospeltruth.net/lawsonbio.htm
[8] See Acts 16:30
[9] Riss and Riss, *Images of Revival*, p. 13

hitting the streets and slums. Most of the Salvation Army's early evangelists were converted in pubs and brothels.[10] Their motto was "Blood & Fire" – the blood spoke of the salvation giving-blood of Jesus, and the fire spoke of the revival-fire of the Holy Spirit.

During the Welsh revival, jails, bars, and brothels were emptied. It's even reported that a police station closed down so the policemen could pursue a new career of being a men's gospel choir group![11]

Society was being changed.

Revival Brings Real Love among Brothers and Sisters in Christ

During the Azusa Street Revival, which blew in half-a-century before the U.S. Civil Rights Movement, in the heat of racial prejudice, the headline in the newspaper read, "Whites and Blacks Mix in a Religious Frenzy."[12]

From that frenzy was birthed over a million Pentecostal churches![13]

When the early church was in revival, there was so much love, people started joyfully selling their possessions to care for each other![14] When you are in revival, you are free from the chokehold of bitterness and strife, and instead you are overflowing with God's love, even for your enemies.

After I experienced the revival fire of the Holy Spirit, I was so possessed by the love and compassion of the Lord, that I

---

[10] http://www.pentecostalpioneers.org/WilliamBooth.html
[11] http://www.theologicalstudies.org.uk/article_welshrevival.html
[12] Michael Brown, *A Time for Holy Fire*, p. 129
[13] Vinson Synan, *An Eyewitness Remembers the Century of the Holy Spirit*, p. 157
[14] See Acts 2:47

Living in Ever-Increasing Revival

spent hours a day, compassionately interceding for those who hated me and betrayed me. God's supernatural love flowed from my heart like a rushing river.

"God's love has been poured into our hearts through the Holy Spirit who has been given to us" (Romans 5:5 ESV).

In Revival, Powerful Encounters with God Happen

Do you know how the Quakers and Shakers got their name? The presence of God would come so powerfully upon them, they would quake and shake.

Of course, I'm not saying that if you don't quake and shake you are not in revival. But, I do believe that when the Holy Spirit invades our lives in a powerful way, unusual things can happen.

In case you have forgotten, God is actually the most powerful being in the entire universe. And when He is at work in the hearts of people, it's not always cute and tidy, but can be dramatic.

> *Revival first explodes in the heart, then it goes out into world.*

When I first experienced the Holy Spirit, one tear-drop didn't fall from each eye. I cried my eyes out for three hours, and I had a "snot festival".

It wasn't pretty.

It was wild!

But I have never been the same after that encounter with God. Before the Holy Spirit rocked my world, Jesus was just a rumor. Afterward, Jesus became reality.

NEVER BURN OUT: Discover the Reality of your Identity

Recently, while I was ministering at a youth service for a large church, the glory of God came so powerfully that many of the youth could no longer stand. They were overwhelmed by the presence of God. After the service, a number of them with tear-filled eyes shared with me about how they actually saw Jesus, and how He personally ministered to them while they were laid out on the hard tile floor! In revival, alarming and exhilarating encounters with the Lord are normal.

In Revival, There Are Supernatural Manifestations of the Gifts of the Spirit

We see all the wonderful gifts of the Spirit being manifested in the book of Acts, as the Church was born in revival.

During the early revival days of the Quakers, the gifts of healing, prophecy, and tongues happened regularly.[15]

When persecution hit the Christians in France, a group of them escaped to the Cevennes mountains, and revival broke out! They became known as the French Prophets, because miracles, healing, prophesy, and tongues were the norm in their lives.

When you are in revival, you will be used by the Holy Spirit in such supernatural ways, that the people around you will encounter the power of God! When my friends and I started experiencing revival fire, we started going to emergency rooms for fun. I stood in front of all those in the waiting room, and told them why we had come; that we were here to heal the sick in the name of Jesus. One day, we saw a lady who had her ankle broken in three places get out of her wheelchair and walk gracefully in front of fifty bug-eyed spectators. Revival was in the air!

---

[15] Charles Chauncy, *Seasonable Thoughts on the State of Religion in New England*, p. 126-129

Living in Ever-Increasing Revival

In Revival, People Find a Great Love for the Bible

Before the Welsh revival, Bibles were regarded as dead stock, but when revival broke out, bookstores began to sell out of Bibles![16] People left the bookstores with their new Bibles, as if they were five-karat diamonds.

During the Great Awakening, Jonathan Edwards wrote,

"The Bible was such a new book. Texts that had been read a thousand times appeared with such fresh and novel interest that even old saints were tempted to think that they had never seen them before, and regarded them with strange wonder."[17]

When you are in revival, you are not trading in the Bible for radical spiritual experiences, but you are having radical spiritual experiences in the Word of God!

Any spiritual experience that violates the Word of God is not of God.

In revival, the Word of God is not just a monument to admire from a distance, but an actual portal that you step into. As you step in, you experience the power, wisdom, love, and holiness of God like never before.

In Revival, People Fall More Deeply in Love with Jesus

John Wesley wrote in his journal about a beautiful conversation he had with a young woman who had just experienced the glory of God in one of his revival meetings: "When the service was ended, I asked her, 'What do you want?' She immediately replied, 'Nothing but Christ.'"[18]

---

[16] Richard and Kathryn Riss, *Images of Revival*, p. 9
[17] Jonathan Edwards, *A Faithful Narrative*, p. 39
[18] John Wesley, *John Wesley's Journal*, January 3, 1760, p. 492

NEVER BURN OUT: Discover the Reality of your Identity

When you are in revival, Jesus becomes your heart's obsession!

When I first experienced revival as a young teenager, my greatest dilemma when I got home from school was never: "Pray or watch TV?", "read the Bible or get high on weed?", "worship tonight or go out and sin tonight?" The dilemma was always, "I really want to pray and talk to Jesus; oh, but I also really want to study the Word and learn from Jesus; but oh, what I really want do to is worship Jesus. What should I do Jesus? I'm in a dilemma."

Causing you to fall madly in love with Jesus is the favorite work of Mr. Revival!

Expect Ever-Increasing Revival

Now that you have a good idea of what revival is all about, do you want it? How much do you desire for Mr. Revival to totally take over your life?

> *When you are in revival, Jesus becomes your heart's obsession!*

Years ago, I remember sharing my heart with a fellow pastor, passionately communicating how I was believing that we would actually see the awesome manifestations of the glory of God that were witnessed by Jonathan Edwards, John Wesley, Charles Finney, and in Azusa Street!

Despite my enthusiasm, he looked unimpressed. Then, he tried to pop my bubble of holy anticipation, by saying, "Do you know how long those revivals lasted?" He jumped to answer his own question, "Not very long! I wouldn't be so excited about that kind of stuff. I'm more of a realist. Just stick to the Bible."

Living in Ever-Increasing Revival

This was definitely not an encouraging conversation, but it wasn't a discouraging one either, because I wasn't convinced at all by what he had to say.

This might sound crazy, but I really do believe that we are going to see an ever-increasing revival in our day! You will never burn out!

I admit, there have been many flashes of revival in times past that came and went. However, I believe that what we are going to witness in our day is a revival that does not fade, but goes from one level of intensity to another, one degree of power to another!

How can we claim such a grandiose thing as "ever-increasing revival"?

The claim is solely founded upon what we see in the Scriptures. I'm sticking to the Bible alright, because that's what true realists do! This is what the Scriptures tell us about the Christian life:

> "And we, who with unveiled faces all reflect the Lord's glory, are being transformed into his likeness with ever-increasing glory, which comes from the Lord, who is the Spirit" (2 Corinthians 3:18 NIV).

> "... changed into the same image from glory to glory, [even] as by the Spirit of the Lord" (2 Corinthians 3:18b KJV).

> "From one degree of glory to another. For this comes from the Lord who is the Spirit" (2 Corinthians 3:18b ESV).

NEVER BURN OUT: Discover the Reality of your Identity

The Word of God is the will of God. So, I've never prayed about whether it was God's will for me to murder because the Word of God is clear that murder is not God's will.

Likewise, in this verse, we see God's will for our lives and His Church: ever-increasing glory – going from glory to glory, from one degree of glory to another! We don't need to question it; we should not doubt it. Rather, we get to fully embrace it, expect it, and experience it.

Sticking to the Bible, I do not believe that it was ever God's perfect will for revivals to burn out, but rather go from glory to glory!

Jesus taught us to pray for God's will to be done on earth as it is in heaven.[19]

Do people burn out in heaven?

I doubt it.

Heaven is a place where God's will is always done.

In heaven, the four living creatures around the throne of God declare "Holy!" over and over again. Why? Are they pre-programmed or ever-fascinated?

This is how I see it: they are chilling around the throne, and they get hit with the glory of God the size of a golf ball. They react by shouting, "Holy!" When they barely recover from shouting "Holy!" that's when they get hit with the glory of God that's the size of a tennis ball. They respond by exclaiming, "Holy!" Then it comes in the size of a volley ball, then basketball, then beach ball, then a hot air balloon!

They are continuously experiencing ever-increasing glory!

Shouldn't that be our reality as well?

---
[19] See Matthew 6:10

Living in Ever-Increasing Revival

God's will for us is not burn-out, but an ever-increasing fascination with Him. God's will is not that we decrease or digress, but that we increase and progress in revival!

Jesus rebuked the church in Ephesus for allowing their church to lose their first love,[20] and called them to repent! This tells us that Jesus hates it when revival dies.

The only kind of life that Jesus desires for us is ever-increasing revival.

That's what He died for. I'm not naively implying that we will never have any battles to fight. But, even with each battle, God wants to take you to another level of glory.

- He wants us to experience more of His joy and pleasure, so we can experience heaven's oxygen.
- He wants us to have a greater impact upon this world, so more souls can come into heaven.
- He wants us to to bring more justice to society, until earth looks like heaven.
- He wants us to grow in our love for our brothers and sisters in Christ, so the Church can represent heaven better.
- He wants us to have more and more powerful encounters with Him, so heaven would become more real to us.
- He wants us to have love for His Word that is ever-deepening – so we would experience the flooding of heavenly revelation.
- He wants us to be more and more in love with Jesus – the Lord of Heaven.

---

[20] See Revelation 2:4

NEVER BURN OUT: Discover the Reality of your Identity

We are called to "live by faith, not by sight" (1 Corinthians 5:7 NIV).

That means that even though we can "see" in the history books that every revival eventually burned out, we will not let that discourage us.

We are called to believe that ever-increasing revival is God's will for our lives, and that we will only go from one degree of glory to another! Do you believe?

Jesus said, "According to your faith be it done to you" (Matthew 9:29 NIV).

You might be wondering, "If ever-increasing revival is God's will for us, why do so many Christians experience burn out? Why do many Christians start off on fire for God, but start experiencing ever-decreasing glory?"

These are the questions we will tackle throughout the remainder of this book.

Chapter 2

Know Your True Identity

Do you remember Nancy Kerrigan, the Figure Skater? In 1994, Nancy Kerrigan had just finished her practice session for the U.S. Figure-Skating Championship. She had won first place the year before, and was expected to win it all over again!

As she walked off the ice and was heading into the locker room, a big man – who had a large black baton – rushed at her out of nowhere, and whacked her leg multiple times, attempting to break it, and then took off like a chicken!

The cameramen showed up in the hallways shortly after her brutal beating, and filmed Nancy sobbing in pain and mourning because she wouldn't be able to compete anymore.

Nancy had everything it took to win the championship. She was born to skate, and worked very hard to be a good steward of her God-given talent, but now in an instant, everything changed.

NEVER BURN OUT: Discover the Reality of your Identity

As strong legs are to a figure-skater, so is a strong understanding of one's identity to the Christian.

For obvious reasons, Satan will attempt to cripple your understanding of who you truly are, because he is afraid of what you can do if you have a healthy, un-mutilated understanding of who you are.

> *No matter how hard you work at perfecting your Christian duties, without strong faith in your Christian identity you will fall short of your potential.*

It doesn't matter how hard you work at perfecting your Christian duties; without strong faith in your Christian identity you will fall short of your potential.

How I Burned Out

I grew up in the church, learned all the Bible stories, and so on, but I never experienced the glory of God. Going through the motions of Christianity without the glory of God is like strumming a guitar without strings – pathetic.

I quickly lost interest in the things of God and gained more interest in the age-old art of sin, and rapidly developed my skills. But, my promising career as a sinner came to an abrupt end in the winter of 1997. My sister invited me to her church where revival was in the atmosphere.

For the first time in my life, I experienced the manifest presence and power of God.

I remember this defining moment as if it were yesterday. His grace overtook me. I wept uncontrollably because I was so overwhelmed by God. My stone-cold heart helplessly melted under the fire of God's love. I remember feeling this electricity-like

Know Your True Identity

power surge through my body, causing a tingling and numbing sensation from head to toe. I was radically born-again and filled with the Holy Spirit!

After this encounter, all I wanted to do was please the Lord. I wanted to serve God with everything! So, I pretty much lived at church. And at church, I was bombarded with commandments. I was told what Christians must do and not do. I was told to pray at least one hour a day; to watch no more than ten minutes of television a day; read ten chapters of the Bible a day; while not neglecting to invite people to church and share my faith regularly, all the while making sure there was not even a hint of sin in my life.

My fresh born-again zeal made me want to rise to the challenge, and not only did I do a pretty good job with all those things, I went ballistic doing all my Christian duties with an intensity that far surpassed anyone I knew! Since I had just experienced the love of God and the fire of the Holy Spirit in such a life-transforming way, I was initially successful in living up to these new responsibilities.

However, after about four years of this work-oriented Christianity, my zeal started to subside. I vividly recall hating myself for allowing my zeal to drop.

The sense of condemnation shoved out the sense of God's presence, and I felt like God was a million miles away. Little did I know that this feeling of separation was self-inflicted and all in my confused head.

When my zeal fell to an all-time low, I was still forcefully trying to live up to all the Christian responsibilities that I'd been taught, but that "first love" was gone!

The boat of my Christian life had just lost its motor, and now, I had to paddle. I was paddling in self-effort, joylessly.

NEVER BURN OUT: Discover the Reality of your Identity

Soon, I didn't have the strength to paddle anymore, and it wasn't just me.

This has happened to many other Christians, I'm sure.

In hindsight, I can see what my real problem was, and how I went wrong. You see, I was bombarded with truck-loads of information regarding what I must do and not do, but I had a thimble-full of revelation regarding my true identity as a Christian.

So, I had a Ph.D. when it came to my Christian duties, but I was a preschooler when it came to understanding my born-again identity.

I was the Sherlock Holmes when it came to detecting sins in my life and the lives of others, but I was almost blind when it came to seeing my own Christian identity.

During that time, the number one cause of stress in my life was my relationship with God. Ironic, since Jesus promised that we would find rest in Him, not stress in Him.[21] But this warped kind of Christianity happens when we put the cart of our Christian duties before the horse of our Christian identity.

Just as the horse is the driving force that carries along the cart for an easy ride, our Christian identity is to be the driving force that causes our Christian duties and disciplines to enjoy an effortless ride. When we rightly believe who we are as Christians, then doing what we are called to do becomes natural, fun, and sustainable! But, if you have the cart before the horse, you will end up with a frustrated cart and horse.

You put the cart before the horse when you believe what you do is what makes you who you are. No. It's who you are that ought to make you do what you do.

---
[21] See Matthew 11:28

Know Your True Identity

In my case, I had a huge cart with a tiny horse, and the horse was behind the cart.

Sustaining Revival

Some time ago, there were two great revivals that broke out in two separate churches. Many got on boats, planes, trains, and even drove for twenty hours to get to these hot spots. When revival hit these two churches, those churches became world renown.

One of the churches was a small church when the revival broke out, while the other was much larger. The revival in the larger church had much emphasis upon our Christian duties: the emphasis was "Get holy – change your behavior!" On the other hand, the revival in the smaller church emphasized "The Father's love", something crucial to our Christian identity.

What Is the Father's love?

Many people have grown up with painful relationships with their earthly fathers, and so when they get saved, they find it uncomfortable to relate to God as their Father (they prefer Jesus). However, when Christians get a revelation of the Father's love and how loving their Heavenly Father is, it not only heals the hurts inflicted by their earthly fathers, but it builds a whole new sense of security in their relationship with God. Many people get healed of their deep rejection issues as they experience the Father's love.

I believe that both revivals had extremely important and timely messages. However, after a few years, the revival that focused more on Christian behavior died out, leaving the church membership a tiny fraction of what it had been even before the revival broke out. On the other hand, the revival that focused on our identity continues to this day, and its church membership has multiplied greatly. When it comes to sustaining the ever-increasing revival, there must be a stronger focus on our identity.

In the first dozen years of my preaching ministry, I was always most excited about seeing revival break out among the youth. So I would preach with all my lungs, lay hands and pray for youth for hours, fast and pray for days, in hopes that the youth would get on fire for God.

However, last year, the Lord spoke to me saying, "Don't focus on getting the youth on fire! Focus on teaching them about their identity, because once they know who they are, it will be easy for them to receive revival fire, sustain it, and increase in it. If they don't know who they are, they might catch the contagious revival fire, but they will have a tough time maintaining it."

The Simple Formula

The Holy Spirit gave me a simple formula for helping you to really understand your true identity. If you are a born-again Christian, your true identity is who you are:

1. In Christ
2. By Grace
3. Through the Cross

This simple formula is worth committing to memory.

1. In Christ

As a born-again believer, your "in Christ" identity is your true identity! It's not one of your many faces, it's your sole identity. I'm not saying that you no longer have a free will, moral responsibilities, and a unique personality – but the Bible says that our truest identity is found "in Christ."

Know Your True Identity

Christ Is Your Life

The Scriptures blatantly tells us, "For you died, and your life is now hidden with Christ in God" (Colossians 3:3 NIV).

If you are a born-again Christian, the old "B.C. (Before Christ) you" has died. What that means is that the nasty, ugly, complaining, evil, wicked, jealous, depressed, angry, sinful you has died!

Whether you are aware of it or not, your death certificate has already been issued. And, there is no need to resurrect that old person.

You are now a brand new person, whose life is totally intermingled with Jesus! Jesus is in you and you are in Him! Say it to yourself aloud, "Jesus is in me, and I am in Him." You are in such union with Jesus.

The Scriptures tell us that, "the person who is joined to the Lord is one spirit with him" (1 Corinthians 6:17 NIV).

As a born again believer, now "Christ is your life" (Colossians 3:4a) and for you "to live is Christ!" (Philippians 1:21 ESV).

As a born-again believer, your "in Christ" identity is your true identity – your sole identity!

We tend to compartmentalize our lives and think that we have a work life, a church life, a family life, a school life, a social life, a sex life, a secret life, etc. No! That's unbiblical. You only have one life! It's the Christ-life! Christ is your life! You are in Christ, and Christ is in you. That's our new reality!

I'm not saying you are the Messiah, but I am saying that the presence and love of Jesus ought to be oozing out of you when you are at work, church, with your family, at school, with friends, by yourself, and in everything you do!

For Christ is your life!

People ought to be telling you on a regular basis, "When I'm around you, I feel like I'm next to Jesus." You ought to respond, "Duh, what do you expect? He's living in me!"

I remember sharing with someone from a foreign country about my relationship with Jesus, and I told him, "Ever since the day I was saved, Jesus has been my life." He tried to correct me by saying, "You mean, he's a part of your life!" I quickly reassured him saying, "No, He is my life!"

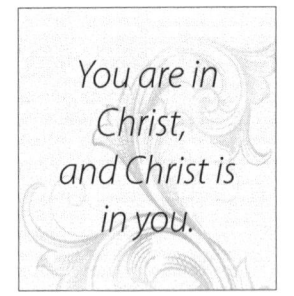

> You are in Christ, and Christ is in you.

Jesus is not a sticker you stick on and pull off! Nowhere in the Bible do I read that Jesus is part of my life. But I do read, "I have been crucified with Christ. It is no longer I who live, but Christ who lives in me" (Galatians 2:20 ESV).

Understanding this is so foundational.

So much so, that God designed water baptism to be a virtual sermon of this reality. Jesus commanded all new believers to be baptized[22] so they could reenact what happened to them when they were born-again. So, as a new believer goes under the water, it represents the death to the old Christ-less life, and when he comes out of the water, it represents how he was resurrected to a new life that's united with Christ.[23]

Baptism isn't what kills the old you, baptism is a celebration that the old you is dead. Baptism in itself doesn't give you a new life. In reality, it's a celebration of the new life you now have!

[22] See Matthew 28:19
[23] See Galatians 3:27, Romans 6:3-5

Know Your True Identity

We've been more than saved "from hell", but saved into "union with Jesus."

In light of this powerful revelation, it's a bad habit for Christians to separate their identity from Christ in their own minds.

How do Christians engage in the bad habit of separating their identity from Christ?

By thinking or saying:

"Jesus is Holy, but I'm so evil."

"Jesus is Righteous, but I'm sinful."

"Jesus is Strong, but I'm so weak."

"Jesus is Anointed, but I'm not."

"Jesus is Wise, but I'm stupid."

This is called beheading the body of Christ! Why are you separating the head from the body when we are one![24]

The Scriptures strongly state, "What therefore God hath joined together, let not man tear asunder" (Matthew 19:6b KJV). Yes, this is a verse about the marriage union, but unlike the earthly marriage union, our union with Christ is an eternal union! So, how much more should we not be separating ourselves from Christ in our own thinking and speaking?

Our new reality is: we are holy in Jesus; we are righteous in Jesus; we are strong in Jesus; we are anointed in Jesus; we are wise in Jesus, and so forth.

You might be thinking, "But, we are nothing without Jesus!" I totally agree. But, we aren't without Him. If you're a Christian

---
[24] See Ephesians 5:23

who is always thinking about who you are apart from Jesus, you're fantasizing.

2. By Grace

If anyone pulled off ever-increasing revival, it was the Apostle Paul. Let's learn from some of his secrets. How did Paul define himself? Paul said, "By the grace of God I am what I am" (1 Corinthians 15:10a ESV).

Finding your identity in God's grace means that you are not going to find your identity in your works! There was a time I did not know this.

When I was perfectly keeping all the rules and being used by God in ministry, I felt like a million bucks! But, when I was failing in my obedience, and was not seeing much fruitfulness in my ministry, I felt worthless! I'm grateful that God's grace has set me free from that emotional roller-coaster.

As we find our identity in God's grace, jealousy and pride will be expelled from our lives. Reason being grace is the great equalizer!

If you are in the sports world, there is reason to feel proud or jealous, based upon your accomplishments. If you are in the business world, there is reason to feel proud or jealous, based upon your income. They aren't good reasons, but reasons nevertheless.

Fortunately, we are in the grace world, and now there is absolutely no reason to feel superior or inferior to your brother or sister in Christ! Grace has leveled the field! Thank God for His grace, which crushes pride and chokes out all feelings of jealousy!

Finding your identity in God's grace is the key to walking in true humility and confidence.

Know Your True Identity

During Jesus' earthly ministry, the religious world He was confronting was not characterized by equality. Jewish men would daily thank God for not making them a woman or a Gentile.[25] Women were second-class citizens, and Gentiles were seen as dogs. But through the great grace that Jesus released, the Scriptures teach that men and women became equal in Christ,[26] and Jews and Gentiles became equal in standing.[27]

In addition, Jesus erased the huge gap between clergy (priests) and laity (non priests), and implemented the reality of the priesthood of all believers.[28] He also abolished the great distance between anointed kings and ordinary peasants, and made all of us (born-again believers) into anointed royalty![29]

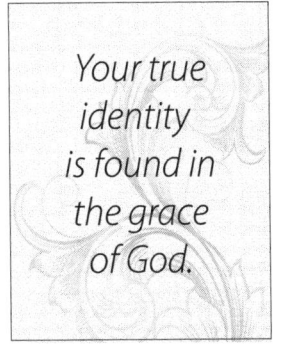

> *Your true identity is found in the grace of God.*

Yes, we still have our separate callings and unique giftings, but we are now all royalty because we are in Christ. Therefore, as anointed royalty, God's grace has now called us to a life of honor and love, not inferiority or superiority; and never self-condemnation or self-righteousness.

"Show proper respect to everyone: Love the brotherhood of believers, fear God, honor the king" (1 Peter 2:17 NIV).

We share love and honor with all people, because we've been given love and honor in an overwhelming measure that we cannot contain.

---

[25] Philip Yancey, *What's so Amazing about Grace*, p.151
[26] See 1 Galatians 3:28
[27] See Ephesians 2:15
[28] See 1 Peter 2:9
[29] See 1 John 2:20, 1 Peter 2:9

If you find your value in your talent, the shockingly gifted people hold value to you, while the mediocre rank low.

If you find your value in money, the upper class are honorable to you, while the lower class carries less importance.

If you find your value in your spiritual passion, the one who pulled off a forty-day fast is highly esteemed, while the one who doesn't fast fails to win your esteem.

If you find your value in your intelligence, the scholar is worthy of your respect, while the uneducated is worthy of mockery.

However, if you find your value in God's grace, you honor all people and despise none because grace declares that "God so loved the world" (John 3:16 ESV).

Do you want to be someone who naturally sees others through the lenses of God's grace?

Here is good advice on how you can grow in that: practice on yourself! The old cliché is right: "Practice makes perfect."

Your true identity is found in the grace of God. Grace is not only amazing because it tells us who God is, but who we are, as well.

3. Through the Cross

The Apostle Paul never burned out. His revival never ended, but only intensified! Paul served the Lord more successfully, faithfully, and passionately than anyone. What was his secret? He found his identity – in Christ, by grace, through the cross.

Paul penned, "But far be it from me to boast except in the cross of our Lord Jesus Christ, by which the world has been crucified to me, and I to the world" (Galatians. 6:14 ESV). At the

Know Your True Identity

end of the day, Paul boasted not in what He had done for God, but what God had done for him on that cross.

If you trust in religious performance, you will boast in your religious performance. But, if you – like Paul – put your whole trust in Christ's performance on the cross, you will boast in the cross!

Boasting in the cross will make you a fat bulls-eye for the power of God.

The Scriptures tell us that for the believer, the "message of the cross is the power of God."[30] This verse doesn't tell us that the message of the cross has the power of God, but that it is the power of God.

If you told me that my friend Tim has a girl, I would think that he finally got a girlfriend or something. But, if you tell me that my friend Tim is a girl – that would be a totally different statement. If my friend Tim has a girl, I can invite him over to my house, and maybe his girlfriend will come with him, or maybe not. But, if my friend Tim is a girl, for Tim to come to my house means that a girl has come into my house! Big difference.

In the same way, if the message of the cross has the power of God, when you invite the message of the cross into your heart, the power might or might not come with it. Yet, because the message of the cross is the power of God, when you invite the message of the finished work of the cross into your heart, the power of God will automatically invade your life. They are inseparable.

Therefore, the reason Christians lack the power of God in their lives is because they lack the message of the cross in their hearts.

---
[30] See 1 Corinthians 1:18

NEVER BURN OUT: Discover the Reality of your Identity

If you declare that you are just a sinner, you are not boasting in the finished work of the cross! The cross tells us that we died to sin with Christ,[31] and that you are the righteousness of God in Christ.[32]

If you believe that you are a cursed person and you habitually curse yourself with negative words, you are not boasting in the finished work, because the cross tells us that Jesus took our curses and blessed us![33]

If you think that you will never be healed, you are not boasting in the cross because the cross declares that Jesus took our sicknesses upon Himself, and by His stripes we are healed![34]

How do you know if you are boasting in the cross or not?

If you give all credit to your obedience for the blessings in your life, you are not boasting in the cross.

If you give all glory to your fasting, prayer, study, tithing, and spiritual hunger for the anointing on your life, you are not boasting in the cross.

If we are oblivious to the fact that the cross has made every blessing possible, we are short-sighted, and unable to see the whole truth.

According to Jesus, truth is the liberating agent. He said, "know the truth and the truth shall set you free."[35] Thus, partial truth equals partial freedom from pride, but when we can see the full truth, only then will we experience full freedom from pride. Understanding the cross of Jesus demolishes our pride like an atomic bomb.

---

[31] See Romans 6:10-11
[32] See 2 Corinthians 5:21
[33] See Galatians 3:13
[34] See 1 Peter 2:24
[35] See John 8:32

Know Your True Identity

Boasting in the cross means that you are finding your identity in His performance, not yours.

See Yourself Through the Cross

When Israel sinned against God, fiery serpents were released to bite the people. The serpents released venom into the their blood streams, and they were dying. God gave Moses a solution. Moses was to build a pole and put a bronze serpent on it. Those who looked at the pole were healed. Those who focused only on their snake bites died.

Jesus came on the scene two thousand years later and said that the snake on the pole was a foreshadow of His work on the cross.[36]

When you think of a pole, you will probably picture a flag pole. But the Hebrew word for pole is the same as a sail boat's mast – which is more in the shape of a cross.

> *Paul boasted not in what he had done for God, but what God had done for him on that cross.*

We've all been affected by sin. All of us have been the victim of another's sin and have victimized others by our sins. We all know what it's like to have been deeply hurt by someone's sin and even bear the regrets of hurting others by our own sins.

But, if you only stare at your snakebites, those snakebites will destroy your life. You must fix your eyes upon the cross of Jesus Christ! Instead of defining yourself by your past hurts and mistakes, define yourself through the finished work of the cross.

---
[36] See John 3:14

NEVER BURN OUT: Discover the Reality of your Identity

The bronze serpent was a picture of Jesus taking upon Himself all of our sins! During that time in ancient history, bronze was what they used to make mirrors. This is prophetic and significant. God wants us to see ourselves through the finished work of the cross, not our snakebites. As you do, the power of God will invade your life and circumstances.

This world and the people in it will try to convince you to find your identity in your flesh, by your works, and through your performance. Your true identity, however, is who you are in Christ, by grace, through the cross. The next eight chapters will present to you who you are in light of these three great realities.

Chapter 3

You Are a New Creation

"Aren't we only human, after all?"

This is a common saying in our world, especially among many Christians. When a respected spiritual leader falls into a notable sin, we tend to respond by saying, "Well, he's only human."

If you are a born-again believer in Jesus, I have news for you: the "I am only human" excuse has expired. Don't worry, this is actually good news for us. We can now live a supernatural life.

The Apostle Paul rebuked the Corinthian church, and challenged them with this question: "Are you not ... behaving only in a human way?" (1 Corinthians 3:3b). Obviously, Paul did not expect Christians to behave in a merely human way.

Was Paul a cruel drill sergeant who was trying to whip chickens into acting like eagles? No, Paul was actually challenging pure-breed eagles to stop acting like mere chickens! Eagles have a different DNA from chickens, and they don't have to act like chickens.

NEVER BURN OUT: Discover the Reality of your Identity

As Christians, we have the DNA of God, or the divine nature; therefore, we don't have to act like we are just human! The more we understand that we are supernatural beings, the more supernatural things we will do. When we got saved, it was through the incorruptible seed of the Word of God (1 Peter 1:23 NLT).

As the DNA of a tree is in the seed, the DNA of God is in the Gospel. So, when we heard the Gospel and received it, not only did it cause us to be born-again, but it imparted the DNA of God to us (1 Peter 1:4b NLT). The Scriptures read:

> "No one who is born of God will continue to sin, because God's seed remains in him; he cannot go on sinning, because he has been born of God" (1 John 3:9).

The Greek word for the word "seed" is "sperma" from which we get our word "sperm". The DNA of a father is programmed into the sperm. When the sperm brings forth a fetus, the DNA from the sperm will have a strong effect on the nature of the child.

It wasn't difficult for me to grow to the height that I grew into. It wasn't stressful for me to obtain black hair and brown eyes. I got those qualities from my dad. It didn't take too much strenuous and exhaustive effort on my part to have his qualities.

In the same way, when you became a child of God, the qualities of God have been deposited in you, and they will naturally manifest in your life!

You might ask, "If we have God's DNA, why don't all born-again believers look like God?"

That question can be answered with another question, "Why didn't Michael Jackson look like his natural father?"

You Are a New Creation

Michael Jackson had white skin, a peculiar nose, and looked very unlike either of his African-American parents. Why was he so odd and unnatural looking? Because he allowed plastic surgeons to perform a number of procedures on him. The reason why many Christians aren't reflecting their heavenly Father in the way they naturally should is simply because Satan has used his deceptions to perform a number of nasty surgeries on them. The tools that Satan uses are lies and more lies.

Did you know that every Christian who is born of God can walk in the qualities of God, as long as we refuse to believe in the lies of the enemy?

This entire book is dedicated toward un-doing any surgical operations that the enemy might have succeeded in performing, so we can really be the children of God who manifest the nature of our Daddy!

The Scriptures tell us, "Put on your new nature, created to be like God" (Ephesians 4:24 NLT). Paul wasn't telling Christians to put on something that they didn't have, in the same way someone might instruct a bum on the street who owns only a T-shirt and jeans to put on an Armani suit. It was the total opposite – Paul was encouraging believers to put on, or display, what they did have – a new nature!

Batman vs. Spiderman

The clearest passage in all the Bible regarding our new nature, is, "Therefore, if anyone is in Christ, the new creation has come: The old has gone, the new is here!" (2 Corinthians 5:17 NIV). That word "new" in the original language is "kainos"- which speaks of being new in essence or nature.[37] It is not speaking of

---

[37] http://www.studylight.org/lex/grk/view.cgi?number=2537

NEVER BURN OUT: Discover the Reality of your Identity

someone who continues to have the same nature but with more tools to do what he needs to do.

You see, when Bruce Wayne turns into Batman, that is not a "kainos" transformation. His nature hasn't changed, he just has more tools. By the way, religion just gives you more tools: they tell you how to live, they give you a list of rules to follow, they pressure you to follow certain "spiritual disciplines," they indoctrinate you with enticing teachings, but at the end of the day, no religion can transform your nature! Only Jesus!

> *If anyone is in Christ, the new creation has come: The old has gone, the new is here!*

They might be able to tweak your life to some degree, but not your nature. Bruce Wayne's life is a bit different when he's Batman, but his nature is the same. Batman is popular because he is an example of what an ordinary human being can do – with fiery passion and awesome equipment. Likewise, religion is popular because people want to boast about their passion, about the new religious teachings that have equipped them, and about what they were able to accomplish as a normal human being.

However, you are not Batman.

A better personification of who you are is Spiderman.

Peter Parker was just an ordinary human being; but one day, through a life-changing encounter, his nature was transformed! He now had supernatural abilities that were built in him. He no longer had human DNA, but was an alien! Peter Parker became a new creation – so to speak.

You Are a New Creation

You see, Christian life is not about giving it your best to be good as a human being. Christian life is about having your total nature infused with the life of God! Do not be ignorant of who you are; don't limit yourself by claiming the lie that you are merely human.

You are a new creation who has the full ability to do the works that Jesus did,[38] because you are not bound to human limitations anymore. By the way, you also have "God-senses."[39] You can hear the voice of God. You can receive wisdom and revelation from the Holy Spirit! Never insult yourself by saying you are not prophetic – your nature is changed!

As I was on my way to minister in one of the largest churches in Haiti, I had a vision of a man stepping off the sidewalk and being hit by a car. The Holy Spirit spoke to me: "There is someone in the congregation who has been hit by a car and has not fully been healed." He told me to call this person out when I finished preaching and to pray for him. Then he gave me another vision of a construction worker falling off a ladder while working and being hurt. The Holy Spirit said, "Call this man out to the front and pray for him as well." The Lord explained that as I called out these two men, the faith level in the building would go to another level, so that when I led the congregation in a corporate prayer for healing, many miracles would take place all across the sanctuary. Everything happened just as He showed it to me.

I cannot take the credit for those words of knowledge or those miracles, because in Christ, by grace, and through the cross, I've been graciously given a new nature that has the capability to exercise God senses and God powers. I give all

---
[38] See John 14:12
[39] See John 10:27

glory to God for making me into a new creation who He can flow through.

Batman has more boasting rights than Spiderman because Batman worked his tail off and used his own brilliance to get what he got; while Spiderman stumbled upon it. Yes, Spiderman matured in his abilities, as we do ours, but he got everything he got by being zapped!

Again, we are more like Spiderman in this sense, because we stumbled into the grace of God that has zapped us with all the power of the cross and the resurrection of Christ, making us into glorious new creations! Like Spiderman, you have new senses and abilities built into you!

> "Truly, truly, I say to you, he who believes in Me, the works that I do, he will do also; and greater works than these he will do; because I go to the Father" – Jesus (John 14:12 NASB).

> "My sheep hear my voice, and I know them, and they follow Me" – Jesus (John 10:27 NASB).

Why New Creations Sin

You might be wondering, "Is it possible to sin even after we become new creations with a new nature?"

It is absolutely possible for new creations to sin. However, before we were born again, sinning was our nature, but now it is contrary to our nature. We no longer have the ability to enjoy sin like we used to.

Let me illustrate. Is it possible for a fish to jump out of water onto the land? Of course it is.

A bird can tempt the fish to come up on the land, and the

You Are a New Creation

fish can be stupid for a second and listen to the bird. When the fish comes up on the land, there is a rush of excitement at first, because he's doing something new; but after he's on the land, he's flapping miserably, and longs to go back into the water! Just like a fish is happy in water because of its nature, the new creation is happiest in the presence of God and walking in holiness because of their new nature. When we do get tempted by the devil and sin, we might find it exciting initially, but it will not provide the lasting satisfaction to our spirit because we have a new nature!

Bayless Conley was a young hippie heavily addicted to drugs and alcohol.[40] His search for truth drove him to dabble in the occult and other forms of counterfeit spirituality. Then, through the witness of a twelve-year-old boy, he became a brand new creation with a new nature. However, shortly after he became saved, out of habit he picked up a bottle of beer and started sipping it. But, after a few sips, it hit him like a ton of bricks: "I don't need this anymore!" He tossed the bottle.

Today, ten thousand people call him their pastor and millions around the world have heard him preach the gospel on television.

There are so many negative habits that we don't need anymore, because we are a new creation with a new nature. As new creations, we don't need depression, anger, anxiety, lust, greed, gossip, or any other sin anymore!

If you have been carrying excess baggage, let it hit you like a ton of bricks, "I don't need this anymore!"

You Have a Brand New Heart

As new creations with a divine nature, we have received a new heart by the Holy Spirit. When the Holy Spirit took

---
[40] Story taken from "Is This the Same Man?" VHS, Cottonwood Christian Center

permanent residence within us, our hearts were transformed! This is prophecy fulfilled.

Ezekiel prophesied of the day when the Holy Spirit would do such a work in our hearts saying, "And I will give you a new heart, and I will put a new spirit in you. I will take out your stony, stubborn heart and give you a tender, responsive heart" (Ezekiel 36:26 NLT). Along those same lines, Jeremiah prophesied the Word of the Lord saying, "I will give them a heart to know me" (Jeremiah 24:7a NIV).

> As new creations with a divine nature, we have received a new heart by the Holy Spirit.

It's been said that the heart of the matter is the matter of the heart, and thank God that we have been given a heart transplant by the Holy Spirit![41] Paul described the work of the Spirit in our hearts as the "circumcision of the heart" (Romans 2:9).

The Christian life is not about dreadfully forcing ourselves to obey God's rules, but it's about receiving a new heart that naturally desires to obey God and to please Him.

The writer of Hebrews states, "This is the covenant I will make with the house of Israel after that time, declares the Lord. I will put my laws in their minds and write them on their hearts" (Hebrews 8:10a NIV). What does that mean, that God will write His laws upon our hearts? Remember, God's laws are

---

[41] When I'm talking about a new heart, I'm referring to a new spirit. It's important to know that our souls – which consists of our mind, will, and emotions, are progressively being renewed by the Holy Spirit. But our spirit – which is the heart of our identity, the essence of our being, has already been made brand spanking new by the Holy Spirit!

You Are a New Creation

summarized by love.[42] So, when we were born-again, we received a new heart that has God's love inscribed into it!

When I got born-again, the first dramatic change I saw in myself was that I was able to love others like never before. "The love of God is shed abroad upon our hearts by the Holy Spirit" (Romans 5:5 NASB).

I really do love God. In almost fifteen years, a day hasn't passed by when I haven't told the Lord that I love Him; but I can never boast about how much I love God, because the only reason I love God the way I do is because He's given me a new heart of love! Boasting about your ability to love is like boasting about your ability to breathe. He's given us the power to both love and breathe, so let's give Him praise and thanks for it!

There will be times when we might not fully understand how we can have a brand new, pure heart. However, we are not called to intellectually understand it; just to believe it with child-like faith.

Of course, just believing that we have a new heart isn't what makes our possession of a new heart true, but rather; because our possession of a new heart is true, we need to believe that we have a new heart.

The Old Testament tells us, "The human heart is the most deceitful of all things, and desperately wicked. Who really knows how bad it is?" (Jeremiah 17:9 NLT). I totally agree that this is an accurate diagnosis of the human heart, but as we've been saying thoughout this chapter, we aren't human anymore! If this is your favorite verse to claim for yourself, you should get on a time machine and fly 3,000 years back in time before the New Covenant!

---

[42] See Galatians 5:14

NEVER BURN OUT: Discover the Reality of your Identity

"The believer 'in Christ' is a new person with a new nature. This means that his deepest desire and propensity of his life are directed toward God. Through death and resurrection with Christ, the real 'inner person of the heart' has been born again ... It is absolutely vital that the believer understand this reality as a foundation for growth. Otherwise, growth in the Christian life and victory over sin is impossible."[43] – Dr. Robert Saucy

Rest in this Reality

God now wants us to show off our new nature and heart to the world.

How do we do that?

When I was taking swimming lessons, they taught us that to stay afloat, all you had to do was lean back and relax. This was revolutionary for me, because until then, I thought the only way to stay afloat was to go crazy flapping my arms and kicking frantically. But our instructor taught us that if a drowning person kicks, flaps, and screams, and goes wild trying to stay afloat, they will end up just sinking instead.

Some Christians are kicking and screaming, hoping that God will give them a new nature and heart. Meanwhile, their new nature and heart keeps sinking all the more as they keep striving. God is calling us to lean back and rest in the truth that you have already been given a new nature. As you do, watch it surface gracefully.

---

[43] Neil T. Anderson & Robert L. Saucy, *God's Power at Work in You*, p. 83

Chapter 4

You Are Righteous

There is a popular saying in the church that points a long, bony finger and says, "The real you is who you are in the dark!"

I used to preach that with gusto.

Those who struggled with secret sins would feel condemned and think to themselves, "I am my secret sin. What's the point of fighting anymore? This is just who I am."

The Lord, however, opened my eyes to see that the real "you" is not who you are in the dark, but who you are in light of God's Word! God's Word tells us that in Christ, by grace, through the finished work of the cross, we are the righteousness of God in Christ!

> "God made Him who knew no sin, to be sin for us, that in Him, we might become the righteousness of God in Him" (2 Corinthians 5:21 NIV).

57

NEVER BURN OUT: Discover the Reality of your Identity

Jerry was seriously bound by lust during his late teenage years.[44] Yet, all throughout this time he had a sincere love for God. He really didn't want to be in this shameful bondage, but he didn't know how to break free. He tried everything.

One day, while watching a Christian Television program, a preacher was advertising his tapes which were on the theme of, "We are the Righteousness of God in Christ." Out of desperation, he ordered the tapes. As he listened to them, something happened. He realized that he wasn't a filthy, shame-bound man, but that He was actually the "righteousness of God in Christ!"

The truth set him free. And the way he tells it is, "I got free, and I stayed free!"

Today, he leads one of the most amazing churches in this nation. He has been a true catalyst for revival. Thousands have been impacted by his teaching ministry.

Shame off You

Did you know that shame never was, nor is God's will for His children? I spent many years of my Christian life weighed down by shame. Then one day I remember having a conversation with the Lord, and He asked me, "Tell me one good thing that shame does for you?"

I thought about it, but couldn't respond. All I could think of was how shame caused me to distance myself from Him, hide from others, and lose all my confidence.

So, I responded to the Lord by saying; "Lord, I can't think of

---

[44] Story taken from teachings "Being Right with God" and "Possessing Your Promised Land" by Jerry Dirmann

You Are Righteous

anything good that shame does for me." He responded; "Then it is not from me, because I am good."

We first see shame enter the world after Adam sinned against God in the Garden of Eden. Shame caused them to hide from God and self-inflict separation from Him. Watching this, God's heart broke. So He went after Adam and Eve, calling out to them, "Where are you?" (Genesis 3:9).

You see, God was not OK with this situation. He always wanted intimacy with humanity, but now shame was serving as a dividing wall.

God found Adam and Eve hiding out, while trying to cover themselves with fig leaves. Adam's response to God was, "I heard the sound of you in the garden, and I was afraid, because I was naked, and I hid myself" (Genesis 3:10 ESV).

God immediately responded by asking Adam, "Who told you that?"[45] It wasn't God. It was Satan's accusing voice that was telling them, "Shame on you!"

> God's Word tells us that in Christ, by grace, through the finished work of the cross, we are the righteousness of God in Christ.

Before the fall, Adam and Eve walked in righteousness-consciousness, which means that they were fully aware of their righteous standing with God.

After the fall, sin-consciousness took over. When I talk about sin-consciousness, I'm talking about when a person sees himself or herself as a filthy sinner.

---
[45] See Genesis 3:11

NEVER BURN OUT: Discover the Reality of your Identity

The root of religion is actually sin-consciousness. Do you know what was the first religion in human history? The religion of fig leaves. That might sound strange, but let me explain.

Religious people think that if God would have favor on anyone, it would be them, because of their number of fig leaves.

And just like Adam and Eve self-inflicted separation from God, religious Christians live their lives deprived of the glorious presence of God, even though they don't have to live with that deprivation.

Religious Christians burn out faster than fireworks on the Fourth of July.

In the face of Adam and Eve's hyper-religiosity and severed relationship with Him, God does something so profound and prophetic.

He takes an innocent animal (most likely a lamb) and violently slays it. I'm sure this freaked out Adam and Eve, because they had never seen death before. Then, God skins the lamb and covers Adam and Eve in the bloody skin of the blameless lamb.

In this unforgettable episode, God was and is communicating these timeless messages:

1. I must judge sin.
2. I don't want my beloved people to pay for it, so I will provide a substitute for them!
3. I don't want them to live under shame anymore.
4. Please, let Me cover you!

This is the heart of God. This is the gospel message.

You Are Righteous

Jesus, the Lamb of God, came into this world, and He was slain for us. As the wrath of God that we deserved for our sin was poured upon Him, His blood was shed.

In the holy eyes of God, sin must be punished, but in the merciful heart of God, He didn't want you and I to bear that punishment – so He provided the substitute!

God met the demands of His divine justice. He took our shame and sin-consciousness so we don't have to live with it anymore. You're covered.

When Adam and Eve were clothed in the skin and blood of the lamb, they didn't need to depend on fig-leaves anymore. Understanding our righteousness in Christ will expel powerless religiosity from our lives. Religiosity always replaces true intimacy.

The most beautiful thing about believing in our righteousness in Christ is that we can now enjoy intimacy with God as Adam and Eve did before the fall. We can walk with God in the cool of the day. We can live in ever-increasing glory, without shame and sin-consciousness depriving us. You see, understanding our righteousness in Christ is not encouragement to snack on sin, but to feast on the presence of God.

Robes of Righteousness

When the prodigal son realized he couldn't help himself anymore, he crawled back to his father's house, smelling like pigs, carrying the heavy burdens of shame and condemnation on his fragile back. His gracious father clothed him with a beautiful robe!

The day we turned to God in true repentance, He clothed us in His righteousness.

NEVER BURN OUT: Discover the Reality of your Identity

Now that the boy was wearing new clothes, he was able to confidently enjoy the huge party his dad threw for him. Since we are wearing the righteousness of God, we are able to enjoy the party, which is ever-increasing revival.

"I am overwhelmed with joy in the LORD my God! For he has dressed me with the clothing of salvation and draped me in a robe of righteousness. I am like a bridegroom in his wedding suit or a bride with her jewels" (Isaiah 61:10 NIV).

> *Understanding our righteousness in Christ is not encouragement to snack on sin, but to feast on the presence of God.*

Notice that salvation and righteousness are a package. There are a lot of Christians out there who, when you ask them, "Are you saved?" will say, "Yes." But, when you ask them, "Are you righteous?" they will say, "Absolutely not, I'm a sinner!" If you are saved, you are the righteousness of God in Christ. For a saved person to claim that he or she is "just a sinner" is delusional.

Some Christians love to define themselves by saying, "We are just old sinners, saved by grace!"

This sounds like a paradox to me. — *Right!*

You are either an old sinner, or you are saved by grace, but not both. Once you were saved by grace, God's grace killed off the old sinner and raised up a brand new creation, who is created in righteousness and holiness.[46]

If you are a woman, and you are wearing a 20,000 dollar dress on the day of your wedding, would you go rolling around

---

[46] See 1 Corinthians 5:17, Ephesians 4:24, Romans 6:1-14

2 Cor 5:17

Not under law but under grace
See Rom 6:23
Wages of sin is death

Power of Paradox
WRONG!

You Are Righteous

in the mud with your dress on? I don't think so.

If you are a man, and you are wearing a 10,000 dollar white tuxedo on the day of your wedding, would you go play in a sand box? I doubt it.

Why? Because what you are wearing is so precious, it's not worth spoiling.

Don't you know that the robes of righteousness that are on you are infinitely more valuable than a dress or a tux? It was paid for by the very precious life and blood of Jesus Christ!

When we can see that we are actually clothed in the righteousness of God, why would we mess around in the filth of sin?

Working for Fake Righteousness

Let's say your dad gave you a fifty-karat diamond. It is worth five million dollars. If you have such a possession, why would you work day and night in a third world country for minimum wage, so you can save up to buy a ten-karat cubic zirconia, worth thirty bucks? You wouldn't.

As Christians, we have received our righteousness from our Father in heaven, and it is not just any kind of righteousness; it's "the righteousness of God" (2 Corinthians 5:21). So, why spend all of our time and energy, trying to work for manufactured righteousness, which is fake and worth very little?

Manufactured righteousness is as disgusting as used menstrual rags according to the Bible.[47] You don't need to work for your own righteousness, you work from God's righteousness that's given to you through Christ.

---

[47] See Isaiah 64:6

NEVER BURN OUT: Discover the Reality of your Identity

For the born-again Christian, righteousness is not your finish line, it's your starting line! Our righteousness is not an award to earn, but it's a gift to enjoy and use.

During a worship service at our church, a young man handed me an envelope with about 2,000 dollars of cash in it and told me to put it in the offering for him. As he handed it to me, I saw condemnation written all over his face, and I knew that the reason why he was giving this big offering was because he was trying to atone for his sin and somehow alleviate his guilty conscience by paying for his sin.

Like any other pastor, I'm a huge advocate for big offerings, but if the motive is to re-accomplish what Jesus did for us on the cross, I'm not in favor.

I'm glad that on the cross, Jesus didn't say, "To be continued... by you ... good luck." Instead He said, "It is finished" (John 19:30 NIV).

During the Dark Ages, Church members offered monetary sacrifices to try to cover their sins. The Church sold forgiveness to their members. Bigger sins required higher payments. The idea of purgatory took off during the Dark Ages,[48] because the Church failed to believe that the cross was powerful enough to put away sin, and God was good enough to count us righteous.

Being ignorant of the reality that we are already forgiven and righteous in Jesus Christ will throw the Church in the dark. On the other hand, though, I believe that the brightest days of the Church will be coupled with this revelation: we are forgiven and righteous because of Christ, His grace, and the cross.

---

[48] Megan McLaughlin, *Consorting with saints: prayer for the dead in early Medieval France*, p. 18-19

You Are Righteous

Traded

Let's say that you were on a soccer team called "The Sinners." Your team's owner was Satan himself, your coach was Mr. Demons, and you were actually one of the star players of the team! You learned a lot from your coach, and brought a lot of glory to your team's owner.

But, one day, the unthinkable happened. You were traded! You now became a player on a new team called "The Righteous." Your jersey no longer reads "The Sinners" but "The Righteous." You have a new team owner – God the Father. You have a new coach – the Holy Spirit.

This is a simple picture of what happened when you got born-again! "He has delivered us from the domain of darkness and transferred us to the kingdom of his beloved Son" (Colossians 1:13 ESV).

Now that you have been given this new jersey, you better get a new mindset. If you still think you are on "The Sinners" team, you might try to trip up your own teammates, and shoot in the wrong goal.

> *Our righteousness is not an award to earn, but it's a gift to enjoy and use.*

So, Paul writes to those righteous Christians who had just been traded: "In reference to your former manner of life, you lay aside the old self, which is being corrupted in accordance with the lusts of deceit, and that you be renewed in the spirit of your mind, and put on the new self, which in the likeness of God has been created in righteousness and holiness of the truth" (Ephesians 4:22-23 NIV).

Positionally, you have already switched jerseys!

NEVER BURN OUT: Discover the Reality of your Identity

Paul, however, is beckoning them to now switch jerseys in their own minds! If you are born-again, you are wearing the "The Righteous" jersey, but did you switch jerseys in your head?

This is imperative to your success as a member of God's team!

I have a question for you. As a member of this new team, what if you forget what team you are on, and you accidentally score a goal for your old team?

Now, you feel horrible because you have sinned. As soon as you have committed that sin, your former coach yells at you across the field saying, "You loser, you belong on our team; you'll always be one of us!"

> He has delivered us from the domain of darkness and transferred us to the kingdom of His beloved Son.

Your old team owner tries to mess with your mind saying, "Looks like you are still wearing one of our jerseys, why don't you just sign with us again – we could use an idiot like you."

Now, all your old teammates – sinners that you used to run with – come to you one by one and say, "We miss playing with you."

But, in the midst of this chaos, your team captain, Jesus Christ, puts His strong, loving arm around you and says, "I want you on My team. Trust Me, you deserve to be on this team and wear this jersey, as much as I do."

"But if anybody does sin, we have one who speaks to the Father in our defense--Jesus Christ, the Righteous One" (1 John 2:1b: NIV).

You Are Righteous

By the way, you are on the championship team!

The Holy Spirit Brings Out the Real You

When the Holy Spirit takes over your life, He doesn't make you into another person, but He makes you more of who you really are.

In the Old Testament, when the Holy Spirit came upon someone, he or she turned into another person.

The prophet Samuel told Saul, "Then the Spirit of the LORD will rush upon you, and you will prophesy with them and be turned into another man" (1 Samuel 10:6 ESV).

As a young Christian, I would pray for this experience and beg God to pour out His Spirit on me, so I could become another man!

Then one day, the Lord dropped some revelation as He spoke to me saying; "In the Old Testament, when the Holy Spirit came on people, they became another man. In the New Testament, when the Holy Spirit comes upon you, you don't become another person, you become more of who you really are."

Pay attention to these three verses:

1. "We are the righteousness of God in Christ" (2 Corinthians 5:21 NASB).
2. "The righteous are as bold as a lion" (Proverbs 28:1 NIV).
3. "After they prayed, the place where they were meeting was shaken. And they were all filled with the Holy Spirit and spoke the word of God boldly" (Acts 4:31 NIV).

Did you make the connections?

NEVER BURN OUT: Discover the Reality of your Identity

1. Christians are righteous.
2. The righteous are bold.
3. When the Holy Spirit came upon the Christians in the New Testament, they became more of who they really were!

Invite the Holy Spirit to fully take over your life, so you will live as bold as a lion, shame-free.

Chapter 5

You Are Holy

When E.W. Kenyon got saved, he was extremely hungry for holiness.[49]

He became a pastor, and would lead long services where he and the congregation would strive for holiness through fervent prayer. They called these meetings "consecration services." He believed that tarrying in prayer was the only way to receive the "second-work of grace" as it was called in the Holiness Movement, which was said to finally break the power of sin off the believer.

After three years of this tarrying in prayer, yet with no real progress, he gave up. He left the faith and explored other forms of spirituality as a prodigal son.

By the grace of God, Kenyon returned to the Lord, and this time he made a commitment to study the Word of God

---
[49] This story taken from Joe Mcintyre, *E.W. Kenyon and His Message of Faith: the True Story*

for himself. He soon discovered that he didn't need to strive for this mystical experience, known as "the second-work of grace," to get free from the power of sin. What he came to see from the Word of God was that Jesus had already set him free from sin.

It was then that he started experiencing great victory over sin. He spent the rest of his life teaching believers that holiness was not a frustrating process of human strivings, but a done deal, and our responsibility is to faithfully trust in the reality that we are already holy in Jesus Christ.

Already Holy

Because of unattractive "holier than thou" personalities, many Christians aren't even comfortable with wearing the "holy" label anymore. Yet, the Bible teaches us that if you are born-again, you are that label.

The fact is that God's grace has made us holy, and this grace is not earned, it's a gift. We are not to be ashamed of this, but rather, confident in it.

Jesus imported your sinfulness and wickedness on the cross, and exported to you His righteousness and holiness![50]

When you were born-again, you became a new creation that has been created in righteousness and holiness. This isn't a theory, but actuality.

"Holy" is defined as: set apart by (or for) God, sacred. The fundamental (core) meaning of holy is "different." In the New Testament, the word has the meaning, "different from the world" because you are "like the Lord."[51]

---
[50] See Ephesians 4:24
[51] http://strongsnumbers.com/greek/40.htm

You Are Holy

You are sacred. You are like the Lord. You are extraordinary. You have the DNA of God. So, if you are living a common and ordinary life, you aren't living out your true identity.

The Scriptures teach us that when we got born-again, we were sanctified. What does that mean? It means that we have been made holy through Jesus Christ. Holiness has already been imparted to us.

"By this will we have been sanctified through the offering of the body of Jesus Christ once for all" (Hebrews 10:10 NASB).

"To the church of God in Corinth, to those sanctified in Christ Jesus and called to be holy" (1 Corinthians 1:2 NASB).

"To open their eyes, so that they may turn from darkness to light and from the power of Satan to God, that they may receive forgiveness of sins and a place among those who are sanctified by faith in me" (Acts 26:18 NASB).

"Such were some of you; but you were washed, but you were sanctified, but you were justified in the name of the Lord Jesus Christ and in the Spirit of our God" (1 Corinthians 6:11 NASB).

"For both He who sanctifies and those who are sanctified are all from one Father; for which reason He is not ashamed to call them brethren" (Hebrews 2:11 NASB).

I've found only two Scriptures that refer to the Christian as a sinner.[52] The first of the two Scriptures has to do with Paul claiming that he is the "chief of sinners" which simply

---

[52] See 1 Timothy 1:15 and James 4:8

meant that he had the championship trophy from when he was a professional sinner. However, Paul retired from that league when he got saved, and so did you. You were actually expelled.

On the other hand, sixty-three times in the New Testament, Christians are addressed as saints. Let's do the math: 2 vs. 63.

It's sad when Christians address themselves as sinners thirty times more than they call themselves saints, when God clearly wants us to see ourselves as saints.

What does it mean to be a saint? It simply means to be holy ones. Is this how you see yourself?

> "We must see that we are not remodeled sinners but reborn saints."[53] – John MacArthur

None of us have earned this. It's been given to us by God's unmerited favor. When we received Jesus Christ, we received sanctification – or holiness – because He is our sanctification.

> "It is because of God that you are in union with the Messiah Jesus, who for us has become wisdom from God, as well as our righteousness, sanctification, and redemption" (1 Corinthians 1:30 ISV).

Using your imagination, please participate in the following exercise:

1. Imagine what Donald Trump's penthouse in New York looks like.
2. Now, imagine what Bill Gates' mansion in Seattle looks like.
3. Picture what the Florida estate of Tiger Woods looks

---
[53] John MacArthur, *Faith Works*, p. 118

You Are Holy

like. Not too shabby right? Glorious, according to worldly standards, right?

4. Now, picture the home of the Holy Spirit. What does it look like? It looks like... you!

"Don't you realize that your body is the temple of the Holy Spirit, who lives in you and was given to you by God? You do not belong to yourself" (1 Corinthians 6:19 NLT).

Don't you know how holy and glorious you are? You are the home of the Holy Spirit! This is mind-blowing grace.

You Are Dead to Sin

God's grace declares that you are now dead to sin.

"What shall we say then? Are we to continue in sin that grace may abound? By no means! How can we who died to sin still live in it?" (Romans 6:1-2 NIV).

In this passage, sin is not an action verb, but a noun.[54] That is why it is still possible for Christians to commit the actions of sin. I want to commit less and less sinful acts, don't you? An important key to success in this endeavor is believing that you are now dead to sin (the noun).

What does it mean to be dead to sin (the noun)? It means being free from both the penalty and power of sin.[55]

For most of my Christian life, I believed that I was free from the penalty of my sin, but I didn't know that I was also free from the power of sin. Yet, on the cross, it wasn't just the eternal

---

[54] Grace Wommack, *The Power of the Gospel*, p. 77-78
[55] John Wesley, *John Wesley Commentary*, Romans 6:1-2

penalty of our sins that was nailed with Jesus, the power of sin was also destroyed.

Believing that we are free from the penalty of sin alone is enough gospel to get you into heaven. But, believing that we have been liberated from both the penalty and power of sin is key to experiencing heaven on earth.

Watchman Nee, the Bible teacher who spent most of his life behind bars because of the gospel, taught that if Christians believe they have only been delivered from the penalty of their sin, but not the tyrannical power of it, they will go through their lives living only "half-saved." [56]

> Believing that we have been liberated from both the penalty and power of sin is key to experiencing heaven on earth.

We are dead to sin (the noun). A noun is a people, place, or thing. Picture sin as your prosecutor, who was viciously condemning you and demanding that you be sentenced to an eternal hell. When you were born-again, a bullet shot through the head of that big-mouthed prosecutor. He is dead to you, and you to him. End of relationship.

Now, picture sin as a puppeteer. Sin was controlling you as his helpless slave. But, when you came into union with Jesus, woosh! The strings that the puppeteer manipulated you with were cut! You are now dead to him, and he to you.

"We know that our old self was crucified with him in order that the body of sin might be brought to nothing, so

---

[56] Watchman Nee, *Spiritual Man Vol. 1*, Chapter 5

that we would no longer be enslaved to sin. For one who has died has been set free from sin" (Romans 6:6-7 ESV).

Do you know what all this means? It means that the Christian has no more excuses for continuing in sin.

Don't bring up your traumatic childhood experiences, or blame somebody else. All your excuses have expired.

Overcome Sin by Faith

By God's grace, we've been made holy and are dead to sin.

Now, God is asking us to have faith in this grace! His grace has been extended to us, and it is by faith that we experience and enjoy what He's offered to us.

"What is not of faith is sin" (Romans 14:23 NIV).

The Lord spoke to my heart and said, "The presence of faith is the absence of sin, and the presence of sin is the absence of faith." The sin problem for the Christian is really a faith problem at the root. As we learn to live by faith, sin will dissipate.

God's grace is God's power-plant, and the way we tap into that infinite power is by our faith, which is our umbilical cord.

"We have also obtained access by faith into this grace in which we stand" (Romans 5:2 ESV).

I do not believe that we need to beg God for the grace to live holy. The grace is already there. The Scriptures tell us that "His divine power has granted to us everything pertaining to life and godliness" (2 Peter 1:3 NIV).

Let's say your television is not turning on, so you call the power company and yell at them, saying, "What's wrong with you, send the power!" The operator then tells you, "Sir, the power has already been sent, and it's flowing through your house; are you sure you plugged in your television?" So, you look at the power-cord and it's not plugged in.

How embarrassing!

Many Christians are crying out to God for the grace to live holy, but the grace has already been sent, and the power is fully available. So if we are not getting power, something is wrong with our connection or our faith.

> *His divine power has granted to us everything pertaining to life and godliness.*

The combination for salvation is, "For by grace you have been saved through faith" (Ephesians 2:8 NIV). Most Christians believe that salvation is by grace through faith. Yet, they believe that the combination they need to use to unlock holiness is feeling shameful after sinning and trying harder not to sin next time.

So, they live their whole lives in a sad cycle of sinning, feeling shameful, trying harder; still sinning, feeling shameful again, and trying even harder, but falling again. Then hopelessness sets in.

The combination that unlocks holiness is the same one that unlocks salvation: by grace, through faith.

If you have a love for the Lord, you will want to get free from sin. But it's not until you are operating in faith that you are supernaturally enabled to overcome your sin. Trying to overcome sin by human strength is like trying to climb Mt. Everest with a bicycle. You need to access the power of God's grace through faith.

You Are Holy

"For every child of God defeats this evil world, and we achieve this victory through our faith" (1 John 5:4 NLT).

Faith Hears

"So faith comes from hearing, and hearing through the word (Rhema) of Christ" (Romans 10:17 ESV).

There are two Greek words for "word," one is "rhema" and the other is "logos." What's the difference?

Logos is the written word. All the thirty-one thousand plus verses of the Bible is the logos.

Rhema is the spoken word. Rhema has to do with what God is saying to you personally and prophetically.

While the logos has to do with what God has said, the rhema has to do with what God is saying.

"Let all who have ears give heed to what the Spirit is saying to the Churches" (Romans 10:17 ESV).

Let's take it a step further to see the difference between the logos and the rhema. The logos is the living word of God. The words on the pages of your Bible, are alive and well!

"For the word (logos) of God is living and active" (Hebrews 4:12 NIV).

However, just because the word of God is alive, doesn't mean it's alive in you. Rhema is the living word that is alive and doing summersaults in you!

Faith doesn't come from merely memorizing the logos, but receiving a rhema word from the Holy Spirit. Thus, memorizing the entire Bible and having ten Ph.D's from the world's top seminaries does not mean you are walking by faith. It means that you have a ton of logos in your head. You are walking by faith only when there is rhema in your heart.

I'm not saying we devalue the logos of God. By no means! We ought to fill our hearts with the logos.

"Let the word (logos) of Christ dwell in you richly in all wisdom, teaching" (Colossians 3:16).

The more logos is in your heart, the more tools you give the Holy Spirit to work with. Let me further explain.

I have a popcorn machine at my house, and when we put the kernels into the machine, the heat will come on and most of them will pop. The kernels are like the logos. The popcorn is like the rhema. The more kernels you store in your heart, as the Holy Spirit breathes upon them, you will see more rhema explode within your heart. It's worth noting that the rhema is founded upon the logos. Any so-called rhema that violates the logos is not a Word from God. The logos must be the number one fan of your rhema.

I always have something to preach. I can preach anytime, anywhere. There is always a fresh rhema word that's alive and kicking on the inside of me. I've discovered that this is the key to walking by faith.

It's not wise to live off of last week's or last month's rhema. We need to receive fresh rhema from God on a regular basis. Jesus said:

"Man shall not live by bread alone, but by every word (rhema) that proceedeth out of the mouth of God" (Matthew 4:4 KJV).

You Are Holy

Just like we need to eat physical food daily, we need to eat a fresh rhema word from God daily. You don't live on bread that's ten years old. That will mess up your health. Healthy people eat fresh bread. If you want to stay spiritually healthy, you need a fresh flow of rhema into your life.

When you have a rhema word in you, your prayers will be incredibly effective.

"If you abide in Me, and My words (rhema) abide in you, you will ask what you desire, and it shall be done for you" (John 15:7 NIV).

When a rhema is possessing you, you will be effective in spiritual warfare. The only offensive piece of armor that the Lord has given us is the rhema. "And take ... the sword of the Spirit, which is the word (rhema) of God" (Ephesians 6:17 NIV).

As a youth pastor, I constantly ask our youth, "So, what's the rhema that's in you right now?" I ask them to share some fresh popcorn with me. If they can share something hot with me, I know they have been walking by faith. If they have nothing to share, I know that they have not been walking in faith, nor holiness.

We are citizens of the Kingdom of God; therefore, the ways of this fallen world are not to squeeze us into their wicked mold. Jesus tells us, "You are no longer part of the world" (John 15:19 NLT).

Satan is the god of this world's system.[57] Therefore, the Word of God tells us,

> "Do not love the world nor the things in the world. If anyone loves the world, the love of the Father is not in

---
[57] See 2 Corinthians 4:4

him. For all that is in the world, the lust of the flesh and the lust of the eyes and the boastful pride of life, is not from the Father, but is from the world" (1 John 2:15 NIV).

Certainly all of us can relate to the deceptive draw that the lusts of the flesh, the lusts of the eyes, and the pride of life has had on us. How do we live above these dangerous traps? God's Word tells us, "this is the victory that has overcome the world – our faith" (1 John 5:4 NASB). Do you see it?

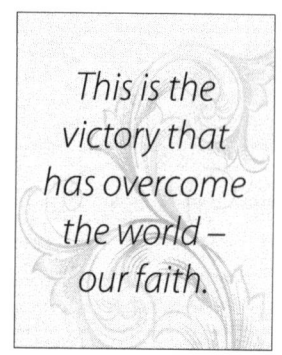

> *This is the victory that has overcome the world – our faith.*

When we walk by faith, we automatically live overcoming the world. How do we walk by faith? By having fresh Rhema burning in our hearts.

How do we see Logos convert into Rhema? Prayer, meditation, and worship create a very friendly environment for the Holy Spirit to breathe. Having a child-like expectation and a deep desire also accelerate the process.

I had a young man challenge me saying, "How can you preach that I am dead to sin? It doesn't make sense. Even though I know I'm a Christian, I am always sinning and sin is a powerful dictator in my life!" I realize that even though I preached the Word of God to Him, he refused to believe it. Sadly, the Word of God became of no value to Him.

> "For we also have had the gospel preached to us, just as they did; but the message they heard was of no value to them, because those who heard did not combine it with faith" (Hebrews 4:2 NIV).

You Are Holy

If you want to disagree with the logos, forget about rhema popping alive in your heart. You will live your life walking by sight, instead of by faith. And worldliness will overtake you as like tsunami.

Faith Speaks

The truth that we are holy and dead to sin ought to so fill our hearts so much that it overflows out of our mouths, because out of the abundance of the heart the mouth speaks.[58]

Biblically, faith speaks. Jesus taught:

"Because you have so little faith. I tell you the truth, if you have faith as small as a mustard seed, you can say to this mountain, 'Move from here to there' and it will move. Nothing will be impossible for you" (Matthew 17:20 NIV).

Paul taught:

"The word is near you; it is in your mouth and in your heart," (note: the Word needs to be in both places) "that is, the word of faith we are proclaiming: That if you confess with your mouth, 'Jesus is Lord,' and believe in your heart that God raised him from the dead, you will be saved" (Romans 10:9 NIV).

The spirit of faith speaks loud and clear, "Since we have the same spirit of faith according to what has been written, 'I believed, and so I spoke,' we also believe, and so we also speak" (2 Corinthians 4:13 ESV).

Who is your favorite preacher?

It ought to be yourself!

---

[58] See Luke 6:45

You ought to preach to yourself, and declare the Word of God in faith that you are holy and dead to sin!

Holiness Is Our Promised Land.

For the Israelites, their promised land was a geographic location. For us, our promised land is everything Jesus Christ has paid for on the cross!

While the promised land was given to the Israelites by grace, they possessed it by faith! Holiness has been given to us by grace, but now, it's time to possess it by faith.

A big reason why many Christians aren't possessing holy living is because of a grasshopper complex.

When Moses sent out twelve spies to check out the promised land, ten came back with a negative report saying,

> "'We can't attack those people; they're way stronger than we are.' They spread scary rumors among the people of Israel. They said, 'We scouted out the land from one end to the other – it's a land that swallows people whole. Everybody we saw was huge. Why, we even saw the Nephilim giants (the Anak giants come from the Nephilim). Alongside them we felt like grasshoppers. And they looked down on us as if we were grasshoppers'" (Numbers 13:31 MSG).

Those ten spies who indoctrinated the people of Israel with a negative report were not allowed to experience the promised land. Their converts were also prohibited to step into the land that was promised to them.

Joshua and Caleb were the only two spies who spoke words of faith! They were also the only ones who eventually got to

You Are Holy

drink the milk and eat the honey from the promised land.

Hear the faith of Caleb and Joshua speak, as they were trying to encourage the unbelieving people of Israel:

> "Let's go up and take the land – now. We can do it .. .don't be afraid of those people. Why, we'll have them for lunch! They have no protection and God is on our side. Don't be afraid of them!" (Numbers 13:30 & 14:9 MSG).

Christians who see themselves as just perverted little grasshoppers will not be able to overcome sexual sin. Christians who see themselves as depressed little grasshoppers will not be able to overcome depression. Christians who see themselves as angry little grasshoppers will not be able to overcome anger.

The Lord is beckoning us to believe that sin is not stronger than us. "We are more than conquerors through Him who loved us" (Romans 8:37 NIV). It's time for us to stop treating sin like an unbeatable foe, and start speaking words of faith and possess our promised land!

> *The Lord is beckoning us to believe that sin is not stronger than us.*

How did David kill Goliath? Was it by trying harder, or by having faith in God? David believed in his heart that he would kill Goliath, because God was on his side, so he spoke words of faith.

Picture a little teenager standing before a vicious giant – the size and weight of a big grizzly bear. David says to the giant:

> "You come at me with sword and spear and battle-ax. I come at you in the name of God-of-the-Angel-Armies, the God of Israel's troops, whom you curse and mock.

This very day God is handing you over to me. I'm about to kill you, cut off your head, and serve up your body and the bodies of your Philistine buddies to the crows and coyotes. The whole earth will know that there's an extraordinary God in Israel. And everyone gathered here will learn that God doesn't save by means of sword or spear. The battle belongs to God – he's handing you to us on a platter!" (1 Samuel 17:45-47 MSG).

That's what faith sounds like.

I'm sure those listening to David thought he was nuts. Did you know that when you start boldly declaring that you are righteous, holy, and dead to sin, people are going to start thinking you've lost your mind?

But, David did kill Goliath, right? Speak words of faith, and you will see the giants of sin and temptation fall before you.

There is one more thing I would like for you to think about: What if David only spoke those crazy words to the ugly giant, but never threw his stone? I don't think David would have lived to be king.

My point is that faith doesn't just believe God's Word and speak God's Word, but it acts according to God's Word.

Faith Acts

The Scriptures tell us, "So you also should consider yourselves to be dead to the power of sin and alive to God through Christ Jesus" (Romans 6:11 NLT). Faith for holiness concludes that we are dead to the power of sin, and now alive to God; but that's not all.

"Let not sin therefore reign in your mortal body, to make you obey its passions. Do not present your members

You Are Holy

to sin as instruments for unrighteousness, but present yourselves to God as those who have been brought from death to life, and your members to God as instruments for righteousness. For sin will have no dominion over you, since you are not under law but under grace" (Romans 6:12-14 ESV).

Did you catch that? This passage is telling us to do more than just say, think, believe, or declare God's Word. This passage is commanding us to act according to what we believe! As people of faith, we need to do more than make strong confessions – we need to make serious choices.

We are no longer under the tyrannical powers of sin.

Some think that they will start experiencing holiness by just sitting around and believing, without making any deliberate choices. That's called dead faith.[59]

Others think we experience holiness by just making deliberate choices, but neglect trusting in the promises of God. That's called dead works.[60]

Both are erroneous, because God is calling us to make the right choices, as we are possessed by the promises of God – which have become rhema to us.

> "What good is it, my brethren, if a man professes to have faith, and yet his actions do not correspond? Can such faith save him? ... So also faith, if it is unaccompanied by obedience, has no life in it – so long as it stands alone" (James 2:14-15 & 17).

---
[59] See James 2:14-15 & 17
[60] See Hebrews 6:1

NEVER BURN OUT: Discover the Reality of your Identity

Do you know how elephants are trained? In some countries, they appoint a slave-driver over the elephant, who beats the elephant at a young age. Then, they use thick chains to brutally control the elephants. The elephants get so used to being under bondage to those chains that after a couple years, the slave-drivers can remove the chains and still control the elephants. This makes the circus performance look more dramatic, because elephants are performing without chains. However, what we don't see are the invisible chains in their minds.

One day, one elephant named Wisdom (not Dumbo) began to realize that he was now free from the chains of the slave-driver. He started telling the other elephants about it; most of them disbelieved, others thought it was great news, but acted no differently.

Wisdom kept preaching to himself, "I'm no longer under the dominion of the slave-driver." Further, he did more than preach to himself, he acted on what he believed and refused to obey his slave-driver's demands. Then the abusive slave-driver tried to intimidate him, but Wisdom just stepped out and stomped on the slave-driver, crushing him.

That's wisdom.

That's faith.

We are no longer under the tyrannical powers of sin. The chains of sin have been broken off our lives. Believe and act upon it. Destroy all the sins that have been enslaving your life!

> "Put to death, therefore, whatever belongs to your earthly nature: sexual immorality, impurity, lust, evil desires and greed, which is idolatry" (Colossians 3:5 NIV).

You Are Holy

We must destroy sin or else it can destroy our revival. Nothing burns you out faster than tolerating sin.

When we make these daring choices as people possessed by the promises of God, we will see supernatural results.

Step out in faith and forgive that person you are bitter against. Step out in faith and be kind to that person who bugs you. Step out in faith and trash your secret sins. Step out in faith and cut off those relationships that contaminate your soul. Step out in faith and don't speak out those hurtful words. Step out in faith and pray for the one who has despitefully used you. Step out in faith and slam the door in the face of temptation.

> God wants all His kids to do great things, but only those who refuse to compromise with sin will be able to walk in the fullness of what God has prepared for them.

When Jesus was walking on water and invited Peter to "come," Peter got a rhema word. Peter didn't just brag about the word Jesus gave him. He didn't just meditate on it for twenty hours. He believed it and acted upon it, and when he stepped out, that's when the power of God was released!

Refuse to Tolerate Sin

As holy people we must not tolerate sin in our lives. If you tolerate sin, God will not be able to use you for honorable purposes.

God wants all His kids to be used by Him to do great things, but only those who refuse to compromise with sin will be able to walk in the fullness of what God has prepared for them.

NEVER BURN OUT: Discover the Reality of your Identity

"Now in a great house there are not only vessels of gold and silver but also of wood and clay, some for honorable use, some for dishonorable. Therefore, if anyone cleanses himself from what is dishonorable, he will be a vessel for honorable use, set apart as holy, useful to the master of the house, ready for every good work" (2 Timothy 2:21 ESV).

There are no worthless Christians; only useless ones. If you tolerate sin in your life, your intimacy with God will suffer.

Although your sinful habits won't change God's love for you, they will chip away viciously at your love for God.

"Catch all the foxes, those little foxes, before they ruin the vineyard of love, for the grapevines are blossoming!" (Song of Songs 2:15 NLT).

The Word of God can't be clearer than this:

"Don't love the world's ways. Don't love the world's goods. Love of the world squeezes out love for the Father" (1 John 2:15 MSG).

Tolerating sin will always do two things: harden our hearts and lead us into deception.

"You must warn each other every day, while it is still 'today,' so that none of you will be deceived by sin and hardened against God" (Hebrews 3:13 NLT).

Therefore, the Scriptures admonish us to:

"Throw off everything that hinders and the sin that so easily entangles, and let us run with perseverance the race marked out for us. Let us fix our eyes on Jesus, the author and perfecter of our faith" (Hebrews 12:1-20 NIV).

This passage is commanding us to do two things:

1. Throw off all sinful habits and whatever is keeping you from fulfilling your life-calling from God.
2. Fix your eyes on Jesus!

Do not ever separate 1) and 2). Be fixated on Jesus and cast out sin. Cast out sin, and stay fixated on Jesus.

This is important, because some Christians think that the Christian life is all about getting rid of sin. It is so much more than that. Christianity centers around the glories of Christ, not the horrors of sin. For some Christians, the reason they keep sinning is because they have their focus on not sinning, instead of upon Jesus.

There was a time in my life when I was only focused on not sinning. Then I just got more religious, and ironically, lived less holy. This might sound weird, but for some Christians, their pursuit of holiness has become an idol. If you really want to live holy, you must never lose sight of Jesus.

Legalism and Licentiousness

"Legalism makes believers think that God accepts them on the basis of what they do. Licentiousness makes believers think that God does not care what they do. Both errors have spiritual consequences."[61] – Bryan Chapell

---

[61] Bryan Chapell, *Holiness by Grace*, p.12

NEVER BURN OUT: Discover the Reality of your Identity

Two of Satan's favorite traps are legalism and licentiousness. Legalism is trying to gain acceptance and love from God by our performance. Licentiousness is living like God is indifferent to our performance. Legalism is counterfeit holiness. Licentiousness is the opposite of holiness.

When we go for holiness apart from grace, we end up in legalism. When we go for God's grace apart from holiness, we end up in licentiousness.

Here are the two equations:

1) Holiness - Grace = Legalism

2) Grace - Holiness = Licentiousness.

Legalistic people are spitting on God's grace. Licentious people are spitting on God's holiness.

It's important to remember that God is one-hundred percent holy and one-hundred percent grace; not fifty-fifty. Holiness isn't the right wing of God, while grace is the left. Holiness is God.[62] God is grace.[63]

So, when you don't understand that God is holy, you aren't missing half of Him, you are missing all of Him. When you don't know that God is grace, you are missing Him entirely.

Therefore, we don't ever want to undermine His holiness in the name of grace, and we don't ever want to undermine His grace in the name of holiness! Because, like two pedals to a bicycle, though they may seem like they are on opposite sides, they work together to propel you into ever-increasing revival.

Whenever a Christian has zeal to live a holy life, he needs to watch out for legalism. Legalism rarely affects the spiritually

---

[62] See Psalm 99:9
[63] See 1 Peter 5:10

You Are Holy

apathetic, but it will lure the zealous young Christian, and turn him into a Pharisee. I know from personal experience.

Whenever a Christian has had bad experiences with legalism, they need to be on guard against licentiousness!

Picture a basketball court: if you seem to habitually hit the left side of the rim when you shoot baskets, you might be tempted to over-react and start hitting the right side! Either way, you are missing the mark. Those who have habitually struggled with legalism are tempted to end up in licentiousness. And those who have had tendencies toward licentiousness, end up in legalism. Both are still missing it. Sin literally means "to miss the mark."[64]

Both legalism and licentiousness are revival-killing, glory-quenching sins.

The only Bible verses legalistic people really believe are the ones that have to do with working to please the Lord and not grieving the Holy Spirit. So, they work their butts off for the Lord, hoping He would be pleased with them.

> *Both legalism and licentiousness are revival-killing, glory-quenching sins.*

The only Bible verses licentious people really believe are the ones that have to do with there now being no condemnation in Christ, how nothing will separate us from the love of God, and how we are already pleasing to the Lord.

We need the perfect blend of all those Bible verses. We don't get to pick and choose which parts of the Bible to toss out.

If you see the Bible holistically, you will know you are pleasing to the Lord already, and therefore you will have a healthy desire

---

[64] http://wordinfo.info/unit/955/ip:1/il:H

to want to please the Lord through your obedience to Him. You will have security in His love for you, but you will also know that your actions are not irrelevant.

God's holiness and grace must never be torn asunder in our lives! God is not calling us to pursue holiness divorced from grace, nor grace divorced from holiness, but holiness by grace.

This is God's will for our lives:

1) Holiness by grace
2) Grace for holiness

He's already given us the grace of holiness. We are holy. Now, we get to live it by faith.

Chapter 6

You Have Dominion

How does a church in a third-world country build the world's largest sanctuary, build three universities, own 500 buses, four jets and 5,000 acres of land, all debt free without foreign aid? Ask Dr. David Oyedepo. Through Dr. Oyedepo's ministry, hundreds of thousands of people have been saved, healed, delivered from demons, and have experienced financial breakthroughs. Surprisingly, all this is what Dr. Oyedepo calls, "stress-free, sweat-free ministry."[65]

He believes that in Christ, by grace, and through the cross, we now have dominion, so as we are obedient to the leading of the Holy Spirit, taking dominion for the Kingdom of God is inevitable.

By the way, Dr. Oyedepo has not had one sleepless night. Which tells us that living a life of dominion, doesn't mean you have to stress out and abuse your health. Today, their great

---

[65] David Oyedepo, *Exploits in Ministry,* Dominion Publishing

church is taking dominion over Africa, and now they are sending missionaries and ministry funds all over the world. They are making earth look more like heaven.

God's Original Plan

If you got in a time machine and showed Father Abraham a light bulb, he would probably not know what to do with it. He and his son Isaac might play catch with it, or stickball, or maybe his wife Sarah would use it as an ornament for their tent. Either way, without understanding the true purpose of the light bulb, they would waste its potential. But what if Thomas Edison was able to give them a one hour lecture on this fixture and why he invented it; and then spent a month explaining to them about how electricity works? Then they would be able to use the light bulb for its intended purpose.

> *For us to discover our true purpose in life, we need to tap into the mind of our Creator.*

Remember, that the potential for electric powered light bulbs were always around, it just wasn't used back in Abraham's day because they didn't know about electricity and no one had invented the light bulb.

If you would like to know the purpose of a certain item, the best person to ask is its creator. Likewise, for us to discover our true purpose in life, we need to tap into the mind of our Creator.

What did God have in mind when He created us? Wouldn't it be great if we could somehow eavesdrop on the conversation that ran through God's mind when He made us? We can.

You Have Dominion

"Then God said, 'Let us make man in our image, after our likeness. And let them have dominion over the fish of the sea and over the birds of the heavens and over the livestock and over all the earth and over every creeping thing that creeps on the earth" (Genesis 1:26 ESV).

When God created humanity, He originally intended for us to: 1) be like Him and 2) to take dominion over the earth.

"The idea of dominion has different shades of meaning, which include ruling, managing, controlling, dictating, subjecting, influencing, leading, keeping under control, governing, commanding, mastering, having power over, and having authority."[66] – Dr. Myles Munroe

He purposed that His godly people would take dominion over the earth, and hence make earth look just like heaven. Imagine what heaven looks like right now. It's a place of love, joy, peace, righteousness, prosperity, worship, and the glory of God. Earth was to be a franchise of heaven. Earth was to be the reflection of heaven's culture, and we were originally designed to be that cultural architect who would make earth look like heaven as we took dominion.

And since Adam and Eve were created in God's image, they had everything they needed to take dominion:

1) They were God's children.
2) They had God's nature.
3) They were in righteous-standing with God.
4) They had the indwelling Holy Spirit.
5) They walked with God.

---

[66] Myles Munroe, *Becoming a Leader*

What does it mean to take dominion? For starters, it means to be successful in life.

God's original plan for you and me was that we would be successful on earth. His desire was that we would live in victory, not in defeat. He wanted us to be blessed, not cursed. He envisioned prosperity, not poverty. His will was that we would be winners, not losers. He pictured leadership, not oppression. This has not changed. Thus, the first recorded words that God spoke to Adam were:

> "Be fruitful and increase in number; fill the earth and subdue it. Rule over the fish of the sea and the birds of the air and over every living creature that moves on the ground" (Genesis 1:28 NIV).

The Message Translation reads:

> "Prosper! Reproduce! Fill Earth! Take charge! Be responsible for fish in the sea and birds in the air, for every living thing that moves on the face of Earth" (Genesis 1:28 MSG).

God spoke creativity, prosperity, productivity, and responsible leadership right into the very DNA of humanity.

But when Adam and Eve sinned against God, we lost what they were originally given. We inevitably drifted from God's original plan.

1. Humanity went from being children of God, to children of the devil.
2. Humanity went from having God's nature, to having a fallen nature.
3. Humanity went from being righteous, to being sinners.

You Have Dominion

4. Humanity went from having the indwelling Holy Spirit, to now hosting evil spirits.
5. Humanity went from walking with God, to being enemies of God.

But at the appointed time, Jesus Christ came to undo the mess that Adam and Eve created. He came to redeem us and re-commission us to a life of dominion.

> "For the Son of Man has come to seek and save that which was lost" – Jesus (Luke 19:10 NASB).

Through His death and resurrection:

1. Jesus became orphaned, so that we can be adopted!
2. Jesus became sin, so that we can become holy, new creations!
3. Jesus took our penalty of sin, so that we may become the righteousness of God in Christ!
4. Jesus gave up His Spirit, so that we could receive the breath of the Spirit of God within.
5. Jesus bore our enmity with God, so that we could be reconciled with God! We can now walk with God again in close fellowship.

Now, we have everything we need again to live a life of dominion.

> "For if, through one man, death ruled because of that man's offense, how much more will those who receive such overflowing grace and the gift of righteousness rule in life because of one man, Jesus the Messiah!" (Romans 5:17 ISV).

NEVER BURN OUT: Discover the Reality of your Identity

What Does it Mean to Rule in Life?

What does it look like for Christians to rule in life through Jesus the Messiah?

If you are in finance, you can implement genius financial planning strategies that can save your nation's economy. If you're in business, you can establish innovative companies that pump life into global markets. If you're in arts and entertainment, you can pioneer music, art, books, movies, media that will ambush people with the love and glory of God. If you work in an office, with God's creativity, you can create brilliant administrative strategies. If you're in school, with the mind of Christ, you can blow the socks off the top scholars in academia today. If you're a mother or a father, you can have the creative wisdom necessary to raise children who literally rule in life.

Whatever gifts or callings you have received from God are for the purpose of making earth look more like heaven.

Some Christians think that we will just endure life here on earth, and when we get to heaven, that's when we will really have fun. I know that heaven is going to be outrageous, and I'm excited about it. However, God's original idea for you and me was that we would rule on the earth. He wants us to be excited about each day, because every day is an opportunity for us to make a change in our world.

The drug-addict is not taking dominion over the earth. In fact, the earth is taking authority over him in the form of a plant. The alcoholic is not taking dominion, but a grape is taking dominion over him. The obese food-addict might think she is taking authority over food by stuffing her face, but food has taken authority over her. The TV and Internet-addict is being dominated by a piece of metal. The sex-addict

You Have Dominion

is being controlled by the human body, which is just high-caliber dirt. The money-addict is being enslaved by processed trees (paper money). This is the exact opposite of God's original design!

Most people enjoy listening to a gifted motivational speaker who makes you feel like you can change the world. Do you know why? Because they are being re-connected with their original purpose: dominion and rulership. God re-created all of us to be great leaders! Your influence is to be extensive and ever-increasing!

Now, I'm not talking about dominating and ruling other people as a dictator with an iron scepter. That was never God's purpose for us. The Kingdom of God is not a kingdom of greedy egotists, but servant-kings. God wants us to be powerful people who extend our influence by loving and serving humanity, not manipulating and devouring.

We are called to dominate and rule in life – to be successful, influential, and creative.

Are you seeing that every Christian has the nature of God restored to them in a way that far surpasses the unbeliever? Remember, it was because Adam and Eve were made in the image of God, that they had what it took to take dominion. Therefore, Christians should be the most successful, influential, and creative people on planet earth.

That last statement might have made you chuckle, because you are thinking about how cheesy most Christian movies are, and how most Christian T-shirts can get no more creative than having a picture of an I-POD that says, "I-PRAY."

Let's just say we have not tapped into our full potential yet.

But, every Christian ought to be a creative force upon the earth. We have the image of the Creator restored in us.

We ought to be creating books, art, music, movies, inventions, businesses, outreaches, ministries, and so much more. We should be leading movements; pioneering projects; building buildings. We ought to be the leaders who raise up an army of leaders. We should be dominating over sin, sickness, demons, and the devil. We are made in the image of God. We have the Spirit of God living on the inside of us.

Aimee Semple McPherson pastored the Angelus Temple in Los Angeles. Every Sunday night she would have an illustrated sermon which combined preaching with Broadway. Hundreds of the top Hollywood producers and actors would attend, seeking inspiration. Her divine creativity, spirit of excellence and preaching anointing meshed together to bring revival to Hollywood. May we see this in a greater dimension in our day. It's not being idealistic, it's being biblical.

The Borders of Our Mind

Why do so many of us live far-short of our potential?

First of all, many refuse to allow the Lord to take full dominion over them. You will only take as much dominion around you as you allow the Holy Spirit to take dominion over you! As soon as Adam refused to submit to the Lord's dominion, He lost his.

Secondly, it boils down to our mindsets. "Above all else, guard your heart, for it is the wellspring of life" (Proverbs 4:23 ESV). The Hebrew word for "wellspring" is literally "borders."[67]

---

[67] http://strongsnumbers.com/hebrew/8444.htm

You Have Dominion

If we don't guard our hearts, the borders of our lives will be greatly minimized. Of course, guarding your heart doesn't mean you wear a bullet-proof vest all day long. When the writer of Proverbs used the word "heart" he was speaking about our mindsets. Therefore, in a later verse, he writes, "For as he thinks in his heart, so is he" (Proverbs 23:7 NKJV). The heart is what you think with.

If you allow the enemy to sow lies into your mind, such as "you will never amount to much...", "you are a failure...", "you can't do anything great...", the borders of your dominion can be greatly minimized.

One hard-working man immigrates to the United States from a poor country with only three hundred dollars in his hands and spends his whole life working at a hotel. Another hard-working man immigrates to the United States from a poor country with only three hundred dollars, but ends up owning a hotel! They started in the same place, but one ended up taking more dominion than the other.

The first man started working at the hotel, and his only dream was that he would be able to keep his job. The second man started working at the hotel, but he truly believed that God had more in store for him. Therefore, he saved up to start a small business. His business grew, so he started another business. After fifteen years of more saving, he bought a run-down hotel that was about to close down, and he turned it into a cutting-edge four-star hotel.

The difference between the two men wasn't their capabilities or even their work-ethic; they both had the same I.Q. and worked eight hours a day, but they had opposite mentalities.

NEVER BURN OUT: Discover the Reality of your Identity

Which man's mentality is more similar to yours?

Do you believe that God has more in store for you?

The born-again believer falls short of his potential not because he doesn't have the resources, but because of his mentality. Many Christians don't have a dominion-mentality, but a survival-mentality.

When you ask young children what they want to be when they grow up, they will share with you extravagant dreams! They will say, "I want to be the President." "I want to be a millionaire." "I want to have my own TV show." They are simply resonating with the original-design of humanity, and they haven't had people and circumstances talk them out of dreaming big. Don't let anyone or any circumstance talk you out of a dominion-mentality.

Many Christians have not written the book that God has wanted them to write, and have not started the ministries that God has wanted them to start, because they are afraid of appearing arrogant. Don't get fooled by false humility. It will shrivel up the borders of your life! Humility isn't settling for mediocrity and un-productivity. Humility is agreeing with God that His excellence and creativity has been imparted to you!

"Humility is just the truth about ourselves"[68]

- John Michael Talbot

In light of what we just talked about, and as the Holy Spirit inspires you, I encourage you to start a blog, write poems, make art, produce music, start a magazine, write a manual, finish your book, start that business. Let's use the great potential that we've been given through Jesus Christ. When Patricia King came to speak at our church, she encouraged all of us to put a video up

---

[68] John Michael Talbot, *The Lover and the Beloved*, p. 22

on Youtube, so we could take the media mountain for the Lord. You could think this is egotism, but actually, it's godliness! We have the image of God restored in us; therefore, let's be creative agents who will establish heaven's culture upon this earth.

Christianity = Sin Management?

Sadly, many Christians think that the whole point of the Christian life is sin-management. They obsess more over trying not to sin than trying to change the world. They are so busy trying to take dominion over sin, that they forget they are actually called to take dominion over the earth.

So, when you ask them, "How are you doing spiritually?" they immediately think back to their three besetting sins. And if they had a successful week without lusting, gossiping, and yelling at their family members, they will say, "I am doing awesome!"

Yes, we are called to take dominion over sin (as we saw in the last chapter), but think about sin as a five-pound barbell. If your obsessive goal is lifting that five-pound barbell, and you spend your whole life struggling with that five-pounder, that's sad. Many personal trainers – A.K.A. pastors – spend all their coaching time trying to rally their congregation to have a victorious week of ruling over that five-pounder.

What's my point?

I understand that we are called to be victorious over sin, but we are called for so much more! We are called to lift one-hundred pound barbells, then move on to one-thousand pound barbells, then advance to lifting three tons. In other words, we are called to rule in life with Christ Jesus, and change this world for the glory of God.

NEVER BURN OUT: Discover the Reality of your Identity

"Where there is no prophetic vision the people cast off restraint" (Proverbs 29:18 ESV).

Christians cast off restraint and sin more when they don't have a great vision from God about what their dominion is to look like.

When I was fourteen years old, the Lord showed me snapshots of my destiny or dominion. Sin became the last thing on my mind. I felt like I was pregnant with purpose. I had to get around people and sit under ministries that fed my baby. And, I had to expel people and habits that were a threat to my baby.

> *You are created to take dominion, to be successful, to rule, to influence, and to make earth look more like heaven.*

Of course my dominion-taking will look different than your dominion-taking. It depends on the unique destiny that God has hand-crafted for you.

Your dominion-taking might look like preaching life-changing sermons or producing atmosphere-changing music CDs. Another person's dominion might look like making influential artwork, while another person's dominion will look like planting a powerful church and being on television. For another, it might look like owning a growing business and helping third-world countries. Yet for another, it might look like being a stay at home mom and shaping the lives of the next generation.

When you are doing what God has ordained for you to do, you will be so refreshed! Jesus said, "My food is to do the will of Him who sent Me and to accomplish His work" (John 4:34 NASB). Food is rejuvenating. People burn out when they are trying to be someone God didn't call them to be.

You Have Dominion

I don't know what your dominion will specifically look like. Ask the Lord and He will show you. I absolutely do know, however, that you are created to take dominion, to be successful, to rule, to influence, and to make earth look more like heaven.

Making Earth Just Like Heaven

The following is not a true story, but a parable.

Let's say that my dad is the owner of Chick-Fil-A. And, it was his vision to see a franchise started in New York City. So, he had a building constructed to be the future site of the new franchise.

My dad is a family man, so he wanted this New York City Chick-Fil-A to be run only by his sons. So, I have been given the manager hat. What's my main assignment? I need to make this franchise look just like the mother restaurant. If I do that, success is guaranteed. What makes my job easy is that I can call my dad anytime on my cell phone. As I'm doing what I'm supposed to be doing, the restaurant is running smoothly. The city loves us. We are taking dominion over New York City.

One day, a mysterious man dressed in an expensive three-piece suit walks into my restaurant and boldly tells me, "You aren't running this place well." I get offended, but I keep listening to him. With sheer eloquence he convinces me that he has better ideas about how to run the restaurant. He promises that taking his advice will make the place successful. (Remember, it's already successful!)

I get duped.

I let him and his crew move into the restaurant. I start listening to everything he has to say and I obey him mindlessly.

NEVER BURN OUT: Discover the Reality of your Identity

"You are slaves of the one whom you obey" (Romans 6:16 NASB).

He tells me to put laxatives in the sodas, rat poison in the chicken sandwiches, and make sure the employees work forty hours straight, without a break.

The deceiver sets up a shield so that there can be no more cell-phone reception, so I am no longer able to communicate with my dad.

He puts a blind fold on me so I can't see how the restaurant is really going. He takes the keys of the restaurant.

Now, our restaurant is in shambles. It's pure ruckus. People are lining up to use the bathroom. Others are falling over dead. The workers look like zombies. The restaurant has become hell on earth.

Meanwhile, all the people in the restaurant see the picture of the owner, my dad, on the wall, and they start cursing him frantically, saying, "It's all his fault!" Was it the owner's fault? It was the manager's fault. It was the deceiver's fault.

Then, out of nowhere, my older brother storms into the restaurant. He punches out a bunch of the crew that the deceiver brought with him. He brings the original manual straight from the headquarters of Chick-Fil-A and starts reading it to all the employees saying, "Do not mix laxatives in the sodas." "The ingredients of the chicken sandwich include: chicken, the buns, and two pickles and that's it!" "Workers will only work eight hour shifts, and will get breaks every hour – plus, Sundays off."

The deceiver sees what's happening, so he tries to kill my brother by firing a bullet at him. But the murder attempt backfires, because my wise brother is wearing a bullet-proof vest, so the bullet ricochets and hits the deceiver's spine, paralyzing him for good.

You Have Dominion

Then my brother breaks the reception shield so I can be in constant communication with my dad again. He also takes off my blindfold, so I can see just how wicked this deceiver really was. Then, before he takes off to go back to our dad, he tosses me the keys again. Not just that, but he also leaves the original Chick-Fil-A Manual with me.

This is the story of the Kingdom of God.

Our Father in Heaven created this earth, and put His son Adam on it to rule it. Adam's assignment was to make earth look more like heaven. Adam was given authority and was to take dominion. But, just like I allowed the deceiver to speak into my life in the little story I just told, Adam failed to kick out Satan, and Adam and Eve bought into the lies of the deceiver. Since then, humanity has lost its connection to the Father, and the god of this world, Satan, has blinded our eyes. Satan also usurped our authority, and has been working to make earth look more like hell.

Of course people who don't know the whole story saw evil, suffering, disease and death begin spreading, and they pointed to the Father, trying to blame Him.

Then, Jesus came on the scene – the only begotten Son of God. And He came with power. He took dominion over demons, sickness, and even nature. He came to destroy the works of the devil.

Satan tried to kill Him, but it backfired!

> "[God] disarmed the principalities and powers that were ranged against us and made a bold display and public example of them, in triumphing over them in Him and in it [the cross]" (Colossians 2:15 AMP).

"None of the rulers of this age understood it, for if they had, they would not have crucified the Lord of glory" (1 Corinthians 2:8 NIV).

He spoke the truth. He revealed to us the original plan of God for the earth by teaching us, "The kingdom of heaven is like ..." He and His staff brought to us the original manual: the Word of God. He opened our eyes to see His grace. And He gave us the authority back.

> "I will give you the keys of the kingdom of heaven; and whatever you bind (declare to be improper and unlawful) on earth must be what is already bound in heaven; and whatever you loose (declare lawful) on earth must be what is already loosed in heaven" – Jesus (Matthew 16:19 AMP).

> "All authority (all power or rule) in heaven and on earth has been given to me. Go then and make disciples ..." – Jesus (Matthew 28:18-19 AMP).

Again I repeat, we now have everything we need to make earth look just like heaven. The original assignment has now been restored!

What is the percentage of heaven on the earth today? It is actually 12.876 percent. OK, not really. I admit I don't actually know what the percentage is, but I know that we are called to raise the percentage by taking dominion!

Exercising Your Dominion

During my rebellious, early-teen years, I broke the heart of my parents on a regular basis. I was under the control of evil spirits. I was busy making earth look like hell, and hurt a lot of people in the process. But my mom fervently prayed for me. She had purposed in her heart to take authority over those evil spirits that had taken over my life. She prayed and prayed, binding and loosing through the help of the Holy Spirit.

Adam and Eve weren't given a shotgun in the Garden of Eden, but a tongue. We have more power in our tongues than we realize, and we exercise our authority by making prayers and declarations in Jesus' name. Nowhere in the New Testament are we told to beg God like slaves, but are called to ask like sons, and make decrees like kings!

As my mom continued in persistent intercession on my behalf, one night she had a prophetic dream. In it, she saw a vision of a big boa constrictor snake wrapped around me. I was near a hopeless death. But in the vision, she grabbed the snake and pulled it off me, and threw it in the trash can! A few days later, I encountered the love of God and the power of the Holy Spirit and broke free from Satan's chokehold! That's called exercising authority! Jesus said:

> "And these signs will accompany those who believe: in my name they will cast out demons" (Mark 16:17 ESV).

Since my deliverance, I've cast out demons in a number of third-world countries, in America, and even once on an airplane. As demons have left people, I've seen their sicknesses healed, their addictions broken, and their peace and joy restored. Anywhere and everywhere we are called to exercise the authority that Jesus has given to us.

> "But if it is by the Spirit of God that I cast out demons, then the kingdom of God has come upon you" (Matthew 12:28 ESV).

NEVER BURN OUT: Discover the Reality of your Identity

How to Increase Your Dominion

"You know that the rulers of the Gentiles lord it over them, and their great ones exercise authority over them. It shall not be so among you. But whoever would be great among you must be your servants, and whoever would be first among you must be your slave, even as the Son of Man came not to be served but to serve, and to give his life as a ransom for many" (Matthew 20:25-28 ESV).

The way we increase in our dominion is not by lording over others, but by serving others. The Kingdom of God is a kingdom of servant-kings – Jesus Christ being the perfect example. He served His way into greater dominion.[69]

Satan wanted to become great, but was reduced to nothing. Jesus wanted to serve, and was given all dominion. Whose disciple are we?

Are we always asking the question, "How can I become great?" Or, do we come before the Lord and ask this question, "Lord, how can I serve today, and in this season of my life?"

"They came to Capernaum. When he was in the house, he asked them, 'What were you arguing about on the road?' But they kept quiet because on the way they had argued about who was the greatest. Sitting down, Jesus called the Twelve and said, 'If anyone wants to be first, he must be the very last, and the servant of all'" (Mark 8:33-35).

In this passage, Jesus was telling His disciples to stop wrestling with the question, "How can I become the greatest?" But, rather, "How can I best serve the Lord and others right now?"

---
[69] See Philippians 2

You Have Dominion

If you are asking the first question, you will not take as much dominion as you should, and you will never be great in the Kingdom of God. However, if you are one who truly asks and answers the second question, you are already on your way to taking greater dominion, and attaining true greatness in the Kingdom of God.

Remember when Satan gave Jesus a panorama presentation of all the kingdoms of the world and offered them to Jesus if He would worship him? Satan was offering Jesus greatness and dominion, and Satan was tempting Jesus to skip the cross, and just get instant satisfaction. Of course, Jesus saw through this deception and refused to sign the deal.

Wait, was it God's will to give Jesus greatness and dominion? Absolutely. God's way was that Jesus would gain it through serving (the cross was the greatest act of serving in all eternity), not short-cuts. Jesus didn't force His way into His great destiny, but trusted His Father to bring it to pass. Meanwhile, He kept asking and answering this question, "Father, how can I serve You right now?"

So many of God's people desperately want to be great, and unlike Jesus, they want to take short-cuts. And, unlike Jesus, they refuse to trust their Father to bring their great destiny to pass. So, they are manipulating others, competing viciously with one another, trying to fight for prestige, and pushing and shoving their way into a place of power and influence. Sadly, they are missing it.

We all have an innate desire for greatness and influence, but we need to trust the Lord to bring it about in His perfect timing. Meanwhile, we are called to be asking and answering this question, "How can I best serve you, God, in this season of my life?"

NEVER BURN OUT: Discover the Reality of your Identity

So, You Want to Be a Prophetic Revivalist?

The prophet Samuel lived a life of greatness and dominion. He preached one sermon, and the whole nation repented.[70] He walked in so much authority that God didn't let any of his words fail to come to pass.[71] As a first-class prophet, he was used by God to raise up kings. He was very successful in his calling from God. Here we are, thousands of years later, still learning from his life and wisdom.

Today, God is looking for someone who will know His voice, win nations to Jesus Christ, and raise up world-class leaders. He's looking for people whose adventures and wisdom will outlive them.

Five years ago, the Holy Spirit spoke to my heart saying, "Many young people want to be a prophetic revivalist like Samuel, but they don't want to serve their Eli."

Samuel didn't become a superstar overnight. He spent years assisting Eli. The Bible tells us that "Samuel served the Lord by assisting Eli" (1 Samuel 3:1 NLT). Eli was Samuel's divine connection. Who is your Eli? Who or where has God called you to assist right now? By assisting your divine connection, you are actually serving the Lord.

Many people have such big God-given dreams, but they don't know how it will come to pass. They feel lost because they don't know what they should be doing. They know they are called to one day preach to thousands of people, but they are flipping burgers for minimum wage, so they are frustrated. There is no need for frustration. All you need is to locate your Eli. Your Eli is who, where, and how God wants you to serve right now.

---

[70] See 1 Samuel 7:5-6
[71] See 1 Samuel 3:19

You Have Dominion

When the Lord connects you to your Eli, serve faithfully. Serve with excellence, so your Eli can count on you. And you will serve your way into greater dominion. We increase our dominion as we increase in our serving, not our lording.

"And if you have not been faithful in that which is another's, who will give you that which is your own?" (Luke 16:12 ESV).

Are You a Merchant or a Servant?

Once, the Lord spoke to my heart saying, "Many of my kids are merchants, rather than servants." Then He explained the difference. Merchants will only give sacrificially if they are promised something back. They only serve with ulterior motives for gaining popularity, prestige, or possessions. Merchants will never serve for nothing, so they will only serve those who greatly benefit them. Merchants are terrified of robbers, they are afraid that their clients will take off without repaying them for their service.

But servants are different. Servants serve out of a heart to bless and love people, not to gain from them. Servants aren't afraid of being used. There was a time in my life when I was too cynical of people, and if I poured my life into someone or some ministry I would ask myself, "Will they just use me and spit me out?" The Lord had to deliver me from that merchant mentality, and teach me to serve as unto the Lord, not worrying about getting anything in return. Will you serve your Eli without expecting anything in return? Can you serve your Eli just because you love? If so, you're on the same path to greatness and dominion as Samuel.

I do have to warn you that your Eli will not be perfect. Eli was not a flawless man. He was a legitimate servant of God, and he was anointed, but he had some issues. He didn't know how to discipline his sons, and he didn't know how to discipline himself, so he was obese. While you serve under your Eli, you might have some servings of humble pie. Don't worry, it won't kill you. As you serve, your character will be formed. It's been said that even though our gifts can take us places, it's our character that keeps us there. The gifts that God has put within you can enlarge the borders of your dominion, but ultimately it's your character that will keep Satan from taking it back.

> Even though our gifts can take us places, it's our character that keeps us there.

If God has connected you to a church, a pastor, or a ministry, do not jump ship over petty offenses. We are to be led by the Holy Spirit, not our emotions. "For we who are led by the Spirit of God are sons of God" (Romans 8:14 ESV).

> "Obey your (spiritual) leaders and submit to them, for they are keeping watch over your souls, as those who will have to give an account. Let them do this with joy and not with groaning, for that would be of no advantage to you" (Hebrews 13:17 ESV).

We are called to love and support our pastors until the Lord specifically sends you out. Mark my words, those who have a critical spirit toward their church leaders are the ones who burn out faster than anyone. They burn out so bad, many of them have an extremely hard time getting back into serving the Lord.

There are some people who will only serve if they have a prestigious position or the church pays them. These people can never be the future spiritual mothers and fathers of this generation. Two women came to Solomon with one baby, both claiming that the baby was theirs. Because Solomon had the wisdom of God, he knew exactly what to do. He asked for a sword and told the two women that he would cut the baby in half. The first woman said, "OK, sounds fair enough." The second woman said, "No! Give her the baby, just don't kill him!" Solomon instantly knew who the real mother was.

The true spiritual mothers and fathers – who will be elevated to a place of greatness and given many spiritual children – are those who truly love and care for people; those who are true servants. Those who only want to serve people if they are given a title, honor, or money are not ready for spiritual children, and they are far from true Kingdom greatness. They are counterfeits who only want to serve if they are "in-charge." They are too insecure and big-headed to serve under anybody else! Even though you might not be "in-charge" of a great ministry, company, or business right now, still serve with love. That's the way of Jesus.

How to Handle Success

Let's close this chapter by addressing the topic of how to handle success. This is a very relevant topic for us because we are not expecting failure, but only success; only dominion. Success is not a scary thing for the Christian; it's to be a normal thing.

"The LORD will make you the head and not the tail, and you only will be above, and you will not be underneath" (Deuteronomy 28:13 NASB).

As the borders of our dominion increase, how should we respond to our own success?

Enjoy Success with Him, Not instead of Him

First of all, the Lord wants us to enjoy our success with Him, not instead of Him.

NEVER BURN OUT: Discover the Reality of your Identity

Let's say that I want to bless my wife, so I secretly buy us two round-trip tickets to Hawaii. When I break the news, she gets super excited. But once we arrive, she gets sucked into the island, and forgets about me. She's marveling at the scenery, swimming by herself being fascinated by the tropical fish for hours in the clear water. She is stuffing her face with pulled pork, and at night, she's hugging a palm tree. Imagine how annoyed I would be. I'd be thinking to myself, "I brought you to Hawaii so you can enjoy it with me, not instead of me!"

Enjoy your dominion with the Lord, never instead of Him.

Ten lepers came to Jesus for healing.[72] All ten of them were given dominion over their leprosy, only one came back to say, "thank you" and to worship. Nine of them enjoyed their dominion instead of Jesus. Only one of them enjoyed their dominion with Him.

Never Forget Where the Lord Has Brought You from.

The Apostle Paul preached the gospel all over the world. It's been said that after Jesus, he remains the most influential Christian to ever live. Paul walked in dominion. The Bible says God worked unusual miracles through Paul's hands.[73] Yet, Paul never forgot where the Lord brought him from. That's true humility.

All throughout his ministry, he was always telling the story of the wretched sinner that he was before the grace of God ambushed him on Damascus Road. He never forgot.

I can picture Paul in his old age, standing before Caesar, with tears rolling down his face, beaming with ecstatic joy, as he retells what happened to him when he first met the Lord Jesus. As we take dominion, may we never forget.

---
[72] See Luke 17:12
[73] See Acts 19:12

Chapter 7

You Are in Covenant with God

One relationship can change your life forever.

"From ancient times, a covenant was the highest form of mutual commitment and unity that any two individuals could express. In the Bible, the word covenant means to 'fetter together.' A covenant bound you for life to your covenant partner. It signified that two people had become one."[74] – Francis Frangipane

David, the shepherd boy from the countryside was up on the mountain with his best friend Jonathan – the king's son. They had been best of friends for a while, but now they were about to become covenant brothers.[75] This was Jonathan's idea all along.

He took out a sharp knife, and cut his hands and feet. Blood was everywhere. David followed suit. The two joined hands and

---

[74] Francis Frangipane, *The Stronghold of God*, p. 47
[75] See 1 Samuel 18

feet, letting their blood mingle. They became blood brothers for life.

They continued the covenant ceremony by exchanging robes and armor. David came down from that mountain dressed like Jonathan, and Jonathan like David.

Years later, Jonathan was tragically killed in a battle, alongside his father – King Saul. Who would now be the next king? Who was going to be the ruler of Israel?

Jonathan was next in line to be king, but when he came into blood covenant with David, he was making the statement, "What's mine is yours."

Some people might have thought that David usurped the throne. Actually, he rightfully took his God-ordained position as king through covenant. A shepherd boy, who had been the black-sheep of his family, ended up becoming the greatest king in Israel's history (after Jesus).

How? Covenant.

In the last chapter, we talked about dominion. So, what gives you the right to reign in life? The covenant.

Jonathan is a picture of Jesus, the Son of God. David is a picture of you and me.

On the cross, Jesus took our sinful robes and weak armor, and we have received His righteous robes and mighty armor. What's His is now ours.

> "Through Christ, God has blessed us with every spiritual blessing that heaven has to offer" (Ephesians 1:3 GTW).

> "(Jesus has) made us kings and priests to our God, and we will reign on earth" (Revelation 5:10 WBT).

You Are in Covenant with God

Why did Jonathan even bother to come into covenant with a lower-class civilian like David?

"Jonathan made a covenant with David because he loved him as himself" (1 Samuel 18:3 NIV).

This was the same reason Jesus came into covenant with us.

> *Through Christ, God has blessed us with every spiritual blessing that heaven has to offer.*

Re-Discovering Covenant[76]

If I call my grandma up on the phone, and enthusiastically tell her, "Grandma, God has given me a brand new download! It's so much better than the old download," she won't understand what I'm talking about, because she doesn't speak English or computer lingo.

When we read the Bible, we see the word "covenant" appear almost three-hundred times.[77] The Bible tells us that we are in the "new covenant."[78] Does that mean much to you? It can't if you don't understand covenant.

In our nation today, the meaning of covenant has been lost. It has become a foreign language to us. However, during Bible times, covenants were as common as computers are today. When

---

[76] All factual information about the ancient covenant ceremony taken from *Power of the Blood Covenant*, by Malcolm Smith; *Shaking Hands with God*, by Dick Bernal; *The Blood Covenant*, by E.W. Kenyon; *The Covenant*, by James Garlow; *The Blood Covenant: A primitive rite and it's bearings on Scripture*, by Clay Trumball

[77] James Garlow, *The Covenant*, p. 14
[78] See Hebrews 8:6

somebody in Paul's day heard that Jesus had come to give them "the new covenant," it meant everything to them.

Today, we have replaced covenant with contracts. Contracts are breakable. Covenants aren't. Contracts are signed with ink. Covenants are sealed in blood. Contracts have to do with your money. Covenants have to do with your entire life.

In God's perfect design, marriage was designed to be a covenant. In fact, when a virgin woman comes into covenant with her husband, her hymen breaks, and their covenant is sealed in blood. Yet, with the divorce rate being as high as it is, marriage has sadly been reduced to a contract.

God's people must re-discover the power of the covenant.

Without understanding covenant, the Bible becomes fuzzy, because the Bible is a book of covenants, presenting the Old Covenant (Old Testament) and the New Covenant (New Testament).

An Example of the Covenant

Quite often, groups came into covenant with each other based upon strengths and weaknesses. The following is an example of what would often occur:

Thousands of years ago, there was a tribe of warriors that we will call the "Macho" clan. All their men and women were at least six-foot, four inches tall. They were experts at war and excellent hunters. But they did not know anything about agriculture. So, no buffalo, no dinner.

The "Harvest" clan, on the other hand, was a tribe of farmers. Their average height was only five-foot, three inches. They didn't know how to fight. But they were great in regard to agriculture, and could grow and harvest crops better than anyone. They ate well all the time, except when another tribe robbed them.

One day, the chief of the Macho clan approached the Harvest clan's chief and proposed a covenant. He promised to protect them, as long as they fed his tribe breakfast, lunch, and dinner.

In any covenant, there is an initiator. In this case, it was the Macho clan. Because of the serious nature of the covenant, the other clan wasn't casual about saying "yes" to a proposal because it meant giving up their lives for the other person or group.

After counting the cost, the Harvest clan's chief accepted the invitation. So off they went to the top of a hill. Witnesses of both tribes watched with excitement as their chiefs got ready to cut covenant.

The covenant ceremony started with the two chiefs exchanging coats. This symbolized the exchange of identities. It was essentially saying, "I'm in you, and you're in me."

The two chiefs then exchanged their weapons belts. The Macho clan's chief gave his hundred-pound sword and his other over-sized weapons, while the Harvest clan's chief gave his four-pound sword and his other mini-sized weapons. This symbolized the exchange of strengths and protection. They were saying to each other, "My power is now yours, and I will protect you."

Then, they slaughtered a big animal and cut it in half. They pulled apart the two parts of the carcass about five feet from each other, and a pool of blood formed in between the pieces. The two chiefs stood on opposite sides from each other and met in the pool of blood.

NEVER BURN OUT: Discover the Reality of your Identity

Then, when the two chiefs met in the pool of blood to exchange their vows, they cut their hands and possibly even their feet, and joined them together for the mingling of blood to take place. (The everyday handshake originated from this ancient covenant cutting ceremony.)

As their hands were joined together, they exchanged their vows. In this case, the Macho clan's chief promised protection, and the Harvest clan's chief promised food.

Then they took charcoal powder and stuffed the open wounds in their hands and feet, so it would leave a prominent and permanent scar. After they were done exchanging vows, they stood on the opposite side of where they started; altogether, making a horizontal figure-8, which is the symbol of infinity (This is how we got today's sign for infinity: ∞).

Covenants weren't two-year contracts, they were for eternity.

To close the ceremony, together they planted a tree at the very location the covenant was cut. The tree would serve as a remembrance of the covenant for generations to come.

Then it was party time! Bread and wine were often part of these celebrations. The two tribes joyously feasted together!

If you were a Harvest clan member who hated a Macho clan member for making fun of your height, you had to get over your grudge; by reason of the covenant, you were now blood brothers. Often, worst of enemies became the best of friends after a covenant ceremony. The covenant changed everything.

The Harvest clan underwent a name change. They were now the Harvest-Macho clan. The Macho clan now became the Macho-Harvest clan. They had now died to being their individual clans. They were now in an unbreakable union.

You Are in Covenant with God

So now, if any other tribe tried to steal from the Harvest clan, all the chief had to do was wave his hand at the intruders. (This is where today's hand-wave greeting has its origins.)

That would make the invaders nervous because they saw that the Harvest clan were covenant people.

The Harvest clan would declare, "We are now in covenant with the Macho clan, you can no longer mess with us!"

At the mention of the name of the Macho clan, the intruders would vanish out of sight, petrified.

If the Macho clan ever got hungry, their chief would wave his hand, and food would have to be instantly delivered to them.

It's important to know that if the Harvest clan members forgot about the covenant, they would get bullied by other tribes. And if the Macho clan members ever forgot about the covenant, they would starve. But, whenever they saw the tree on the hill, they would get a fresh remembrance of the covenant.

The New Covenant

Let's bring this down to our lives. The New Covenant is a covenant between God and humanity. God initiated this covenant. God wanted to have a covenant relationship with mankind. Why? He loved us as Himself.

So God sent a Chief to represent Him. His Chief was one-hundred percent God.

In covenant, blood has to be shed. Does God even have blood? Isn't He a Spirit? King Jesus, the Son of God, left heaven to cut covenant with mankind.

"In the beginning was the Word, and the Word was with God, and the Word was God ... And the Word became flesh and dwelt among us, and we have seen his glory, glory as of the only Son from the Father" (John 1:1 & 14 ESV).

Wait. Who was going to be mankind's representative? He had to be one-hundred percent man. But there was a problem. God's holy blood cannot mix with sinful blood.

So Jesus Christ, the Son of Man, became the solution. Understandably, His favorite self-title, when He was on earth, was the "Son of Man."

Because Jesus was born of a virgin, He did not inherit the sinful blood that flowed from the fountainhead of Adam. Therefore, He was uniquely qualified to represent humanity in a covenant cutting ceremony with the Holy God.

> "How wonderfully God prepared for the virgin birth of His Son. When He created woman He made her so that no blood would be able to pass from her to her offspring. That blood is the result of the male (the earthly father, which Jesus didn't have). Since Adam was the federal head of the race, it is His blood which transmits Adam's sin. In order to produce a sinless man and yet be the son of Adam, God must provide a way whereby that man would have a human body derived from Adam but have not a drop of Adam's sinful blood. Right here is the scientific biological reason for the sinlessness of the Man Christ Jesus."[79] – Dr. M.R. DeHaan, MD

Jesus Christ, the God-man, would represent both: God and man.

---

[79] M.R. DeHaan, "The Chemistry of the Blood" Sermon 4. www.jesus-is-savior.com/btp/dr_mr_dehaan/chemistry/04.htm accessed June 22, 2011.

You Are in Covenant with God

Many witnesses gathered on a hill called Calvary. On that hill, God and mankind exchanged coats. The Son of God wore the sins of the world, so mankind could wear the righteousness of God. The Son of God wore the curses, so mankind could wear the blessings. The Son of God wore the punishment, so mankind could wear forgiveness. This was done so we can be in Him, and He in us. There was an exchange of strengths. The Son of God took the weakness of man, and imparted the power of God.

Now, mankind can take on the might of God, the armor of God, and the weapons of God's armor.[80]

The Might of God	The Armor of God[80]	The Weapons of God
"Finally, be strong in the Lord and in the power of His might."	1. Belt of Truth 2. The Breastplate of Righteousness 3. Gospel of Peace for our feet 4. The Shield of Faith 5. The Helmet of Salvation 6. The Sword of the Spirit 7. Praying with all kinds of prayers.	"The weapons we fight with are not of the world. On the contrary, they have divine power to demolish strongholds."

---
[80] See Ephesians 6:13-18 & 2 Corinthians 10:4

The sacrificed animal was none other than the Lamb of God. Jesus was torn. A pool of blood welled up under Him. Over the pool of blood, the hands and feet of the Son of God were cut. At last, God and man came into covenant as the blood of God and man flowed in Immanuel's veins.

"Christ is the mediator of a new covenant" (Hebrews 9:15 NIV).

All the promises of God from Genesis to Revelation can be wholeheartedly trusted because they are signed in blood. "For all the promises of God find their Yes in him (Jesus)" (2 Corinthians 1:20 ESV). If you ever have a hard time believing that God will keep His promises, look at the cross!

> "He who did not spare his own Son but gave him up for us all, how will he not also with him graciously give us all things?" (Romans 8:32 ESV).

It's party time! Now, every time we take communion, we celebrate the covenant and rejoice in the promises.

The early church saw communion as a love feast where they celebrated the covenant love of God.[81]

> "In the same way also he took the cup, after supper, saying, 'This cup is the new covenant in my blood. Do this, as often as you drink it, in remembrance of me'" (1 Corinthians 11:25 ESV).

Wait a minute. Does this all mean that every-single person is in covenant with God now? No. Only those who make Jesus their Chief. Only those who make Jesus their Lord.

---

[81] See Jude 1:12

You Are in Covenant with God

"If you confess with your mouth Jesus as Lord, and believe in your heart that God raised Him from the dead, you will be saved" (Romans 10:9 NASB).

Don't Forget

Don't forget that you have now died to independence from God. You are never on your own! You are now in union with God for eternity.

Don't forget Who you are in covenant with. Don't forget the promises that have been covenanted to you. If you do, the enemy will come and steal from you. If you do, you will spiritually starve and burn out.

Therefore, we must continually be studying the Word of God, to constantly remind ourselves of God's promises. Then in prayer, stand upon the covenant promises of God that are in the Word of God. Weak prayer is prayer that begs God, "Can you please ..." Powerful prayer is prayer that confidently tells God, "You said ... You promised ... so I believe, and I receive ... thank You Lord." Call upon your Covenant Partner, using the promises of the covenant, and see His power bring His promises come to pass in your life.

> *In prayer, stand upon the convenant promises of God that are in His Word. Confidently tell God: "You promised, so I believe and I receive.*

Look at the tree on the hill. Look at the cross, where the infinite covenant was made through the lamb who was slain. Now we have no more reason to fear. We are in covenant with God.

NEVER BURN OUT: Discover the Reality of your Identity

When David was standing before Goliath, he had no fear, because he knew he was in covenant with God.

David was in the Old Covenant. The seal of the Old Covenant was circumcision. David had it, and he knew Goliath didn't. So he told King Saul, "Your servant has killed both the lion and the bear; this uncircumcised Philistine will be like one of them, because he has defied the armies of the living God" (1 Samuel 17:36 NIV).

Giant-killers are the ones who know Who they are in covenant with! David knew Who had his back. We are in the New Covenant. It is a better covenant.

"Jesus has become the guarantee of a better covenant" (Hebrews 7:22 NASB).

We have a better covenant seal, the person of the Holy Spirit.

"In him you also, when you heard the word of truth, the gospel of your salvation, and believed in him, were sealed with the promised Holy Spirit" (Ephesians 1:13 ESV).

Do you have confidence in the Lord? Do you believe that you will come out victorious over every battle?

"But thanks be to God, who always leads us in triumph in Christ, and manifests through us the sweet aroma of the knowledge of Him in every place" (2 Corinthians 2:14 NASB).

The motive behind God coming into covenant with mankind, was that 1) He wanted to legally bless us; 2) He wanted us to fully trust Him; 3) He wanted us to see how serious He is about us.

You Are in Covenant with God

1) To Legally Bless Us

When I came into covenant with my wife, I gave her legal access to all my bank accounts. She's been making withdrawals ever since. We have legal right to the anointing and wisdom of God and ought to be making more withdrawals.

2) To Get Us to Fully Trust Him

He wanted us to live without fear, but with love, power, and a sound-mind.[82] He wanted us to have security that our God will never leave us, nor forsake us.[83] He wanted us to have assurance that our prayers will be answered.[84] He wanted to impart confidence to us that we can use the powerful name of our covenant brother – Jesus – against the enemy![85]

> *You are now in union with God for eternity.*

3) He Wanted Us to Know Just How Serious He is about Us

Most covenants were formed around strengths and weaknesses. Does God have any weaknesses? None. Except His love for us.

When Jonathan came into covenant with David, it wasn't because Jonathan had weaknesses. Jonathan had it all. But, in his love for David, he wanted to share everything with his covenant friend.

---

[82] See 2 Timothy 1:7
[83] See Hebrews 13:5
[84] See John 16:26
[85] See Mark 16:17

"And since we are his children, we are his heirs. In fact, together with Christ we are heirs of God's glory" (Romans 8:17 NLT).

From Desolation to the King's Palace

When Jonathan came into covenant with David, they were only in their late teens. They didn't have children. However, Jonathan included his children into the covenant. After Jonathan was killed, David became king.

Every time David took a bath, he saw the scars on his hands. He would think to himself, "Am I fulfilling my end of the covenant?" So he began to ask around, "Is there anyone still left of the house of Saul to whom I can show kindness for Jonathan's sake?" (2 Samuel 9:1 NIV).

Then finally, David heard about Jonathan's son named Mephibosheth who was a cripple living in Lo-Debar. Lo-Debar means "desolate place."

When Mephibosheth was just a few years old, his nurse heard that Saul and Jonathan had just died, and assumed that David would take the throne and kill Mephibosheth – because he saw him as a threat. So, as his caretaker was carrying him out into the wilderness, he was dropped.[86] Mephibosheth lived lame ever since.

At the refreshing news, David sent officials right away to bring Mephibosheth to the palace.

Mephibosheth didn't know about the covenant his father and David had cut. So Mephibosheth thought that David wanted to kill him and he felt threatened. But instead, when Mephibosheth met David, he met kindness. David extended

---
[86] See 2 Samuel 4:4

You Are in Covenant with God

an invitation for Mephibosheth to come live at the palace and live like one of the king's kids. Mephibosheth accepted the invitation of the king.

When Mephibosheth made the decision to accept the king's proposal, he no longer had to live in Lo-Debar. He never even had to visit. He would experience the glory of the palace and the privileges of being the king's kid.

Mephibosheth is a picture of you and me. We had our issues. We had been crippled by the hard knocks of life.

But, we have been included in a covenant!

Our representative, the Son of Man, has included us in the covenant he came into with God. By the way, He still wears the covenant scars.[87]

If you have said "yes" to the King, you don't have to live in a burnt out wilderness anymore; you get to endlessly feast on the goodness of God. In other words, ever-increasing revival.

Total Security

Jesus is more to us than our brother; He's our covenant brother. Historically, covenant brothers were closer than real biological brothers. Jesus is a whole lot more to us than our friend; He's our covenant friend.

Historically, there is no stronger and deeper friendship than covenant friendships. That's what we now have with the Lord.

> "I no longer call you servants, because a servant does not know his master's business. Instead, I have called you friends, for everything that I learned from my Father I have made known to you" – Jesus (John 15:15 NIV).

---

[87] See Revelation 5:6

NEVER BURN OUT: Discover the Reality of your Identity

Understanding that we are in covenant with God will fortify a deeper inner-security in your relationship with God. You are not dating God. He will not dump you after you mess up a few dates, or when He finally sees your flaws. He's in covenant with you. This relationship has already been sealed in blood!

Chapter 8

You Are a Walking Revival

When I was in the eigth grade, I was kicked out of my public school on the second day of classes. I was a lost and angry boy. But, three months after my expulsion from school, I met Jesus. When I entered the ninth grade, I couldn't get into the public school right away, so I went to a small Christian school for one year. This school was very strange in the sense that they had students pray before the class started. And even though it was a Christian school, the students were super rowdy, especially in my math class. One kid would yell at the top of his lungs, "I have to fart!" The kid across the classroom would say in a sinister voice, "Unleash the beast!" Our poor teacher, who was just starting out, had no control over the class.

In my math class, for some odd reason, the classmates chose me to be the "prayer leader" for the month of January. I had been saved for a year, and didn't know much, but whenever I prayed, the presence of God would fill the classroom like a thick cloud. So much so that after our pre-class prayer, the students were supernaturally silent for the rest of the period. This happened for the entire month. Our teacher, Mrs. Carleson, loved me! Toward the end of the month, my parents got a call from our school, telling them that I had won the Student of the Month award. As I went up to receive the award in front of our whole student body in the auditorium, the principal read what was written on my award, "Daniel Park has changed the spiritual atmosphere of our classroom through his prayers."

> You are a carrier of the presence of God!

I went from being expelled in the eighth grade, to being the Student of the Month in the ninth grade. All glory to God!

You are a carrier of the presence of God, and therefore, everywhere you go you ought to be changing the spiritual atmosphere. You have no idea how much glory is inside of you. Next time you walk into a room, fully recognize that you being there has radically altered the whole atmosphere, by reason of Who lives in you. You are a walking revival!

You Are a Walking Revival

It's very difficult for us to behave in a way that's opposite to what we believe about our identity. Would you agree? Therefore, it becomes very difficult for us to continue walking in righteousness-behavior if we believe that we are sinners.

It becomes difficult for us to continue walking in holy-living, if we believe that we are evil. It becomes difficult to continually

You Are a Walking Revival

do excellent work, if we believe that we are slobs. It becomes difficult for us to continue walking in victory and success, if we believe that we are losers and failures.

And with that said, it becomes difficult for us to continue walking in revival, if we don't believe that we are a walking revival!

John G. Lake dared to believe that he was a walking revival. His city of Spokane, Washington, became the healthiest city in the whole United States because of his healing ministry.[88] Lake's ministry puzzled the medical field. One time, upon Lake's insistence, the doctors put deadly bacteria on Lake's hands then watched it dissolve under a microscope, by reason of the power and glory of God that permeated his entire spirit, soul, and body.

> "The real secret of the ministry of healing is permitting the grace of God in your heart to flow out through your hands and your nerves into the other life. That is the real secret."[89] – John G. Lake

I sure don't recommend you go looking for toxic wastes, but we ought to have a greater recognition for the grace and glory of God that resides in us.

> "I've got a river of life flowing out of me. Makes the lame to walk and the blind to see. Opens prison doors sets the captives free. I've got a river of life flowing out of me. Spring up, oh well, within my soul …" [90] – L. Cassebolt

This childlike song is packed with revelatory truth – that you are a walking revival!

---

[88] Roberts Liardon, *John G. Lake, Christ Liveth in Me*, p. 9
[89] Liardon, *John G. Lake, Christ Liveth in Me*, p. 357
[90] "I've Got a River of Life," written by L. Cassebolt

Do you recognize the grace of God that is in you? Do you recognize the springs of glory and rivers of power that are in you? Do you believe that you are a walking revival?

Jesus made it possible for us to be walking revivals or revivalists. As Jesus Christ hung on that blood-stained cross, He received the full injection of the wrath of God in our place, and the cross released rivers of God's manifold grace right into our heart!

As Jesus exclaimed, "It is finished!"[91] the three foot thick, temple veil, which separated sinful man from the glory of God, ripped from top to bottom. The glory of God is no longer confined to the holy closet of the Jerusalem temple, but now, we are the temples of the Holy Spirit, and the power and glory of God resides in us.

The Holy Spirit, who is Mr. Revival, is living in us! When you were born-again, you were re-designed and re-destined to be a walking revival. And you don't have to settle for anything less.

The Gate of Heaven

Jacob took a nap one day in a certain location called Bethel, and had a dream of open heavens over him, and angels ascending to and descending from heaven over him.

The story goes on, "Then Jacob awoke from his sleep and said, 'Surely the LORD is in this place, and I did not know it.' He was afraid and said, 'How awesome is this place! This is none other than the house of God, and this is the gate of heaven'" (Genesis 28:16-17 NIV).

Corporately, as the Church of Jesus Christ, we are a spiritual house![92] Individually, you are the temple of the Holy Spirit![93]

[91] Matthew 19:30 KJV
[92] See 1 Peter 2:5
[93] See 1 Corinthians 3:16

You Are a Walking Revival

You have open access into the glory of God.

Why would the Lord invite you to come to His throne of grace, if He locked the door to keep you out? He opened the door! In fact, Jesus is the door! Jesus is the ladder! And, He's living in you, "Christ within and among you, the Hope of [realizing the] glory" (Colossians 1:27 AMP).

Because of Jesus, we can personally experience the glory of God every day of our lives. Do you believe that?

The epiphany that Jacob received regarding Bethel is the same revelation that we need about ourselves, that "Surely, the Lord is in this place ... How awesome is this place. This is none other than the house of God, and this is the gate of heaven!"

You are a revival center! The atmosphere of heaven will flow out of you and touch the world around you, because you are the house of God and the gate of heaven!

Do You See the Well?

You might be wondering, if I'm a walking revival, then why do I feel like I'm the opposite? News flash: feelings don't always tell the truth.

When Hagar was kicked out of Abraham's household, she felt like she and her son would die because they were in the wilderness with no water! She cried out to the Lord and the Lord asked her, "What troubles you, Hagar? Fear not." Then, the Lord graciously prophesied greatness over her family. Maybe you feel like you've been in a dry wilderness, void of feeling the manifest presence of God. The Lord wants to encourage you like He did Hagar – even through this book perhaps – and let you know that He has a great destiny in store for you.

But, watch this: I love what the Lord did! After He encouraged her, the Bible says, "Then God opened Hagar's eyes, and she saw a well full of water. She quickly filled her water container" (Genesis 21:19 NLT).

While Hagar was in the cloud of despair, she couldn't see the well. But the Lord opened her eyes to see a well full of water, and she was able to draw from the well, and be refreshed!

Maybe you've been under the weight of discouragement and despair for a long time, but the Lord wants to open your eyes, so you can see that there is a well of living water on the inside of you; so you will drink in the glory of God and be refreshed and revived!

The well within you has a name: Holy Spirit.

Do you only see your past hurts and present hang-ups? Or, do you see the well? Do you see Him?

The Underground Springs

Recently I was reading in the book of Genesis, "God hadn't yet sent rain on Earth, nor was there anyone around to work the ground (the whole Earth was watered by underground springs)" (Genesis 2:5 MSG).

The Holy Spirit then spoke to my heart saying, "It was not my original will to refresh the earth by rain. You just saw my original plan, which was to nourish and hydrate the earth through underground springs!"

Then, revelation flooded my heart, as the Holy Spirit showed me that even today, His primary will for how Christians are to be spiritually refreshed is not having them jump from one famed revival location to another, or one conference to another.

You Are a Walking Revival

Please don't get me wrong. I've driven fifteen hours, gotten on planes, and paid big bucks to check out revival hot spots and I cannot count how many conferences I've been to. I enjoy those events. I absolutely love to be in the locations and gatherings where the Holy Spirit's presence can be experienced like heavy rain. But the Lord doesn't want His children to only look for the glory of the Lord at some revival center or exciting conference, while ignoring the "Spirit of glory" Who resides within.

I do believe that revival rain can be experienced in certain revival hubs and conferences, but even if I cannot get on a boat, train, or plane to get there, I can and will experience revival because I myself am a revival hub, and Mr. Revival lives within me.

> *Greater is He who is in you, than he that is in the world.*

I can spend time with the Holy Spirit and be refreshed in the presence of God. He is my underground springs of living water.

> "It was St. Augustine who once said that he had lost much time in the beginning of his Christian experience by trying to find the Lord outwardly rather than by turning inwardly."[94] – Madame Guyon

If you are a revival connoisseur who jumps from one hot meeting to another to get your spiritual fix, you might get good at discerning spiritual atmospheres in different locations. But, unless you know who you are, you will not have the faith to shift spiritual atmospheres wherever you go.

Some of our church leaders were talking with a traveling minister named Joshua Mills over lunch. He was sharing with us

---

[94] Madame Guyon, *Experiencing the Depths of Jesus Christ*, p. 11

NEVER BURN OUT: Discover the Reality of your Identity

revival stories from his recent trip to Western Europe. We asked him if it was difficult to minister in Western Europe, specifically France, where witchcraft is rampant.

He boldly responded, "Not at all, because we carry our own spiritual climate." Don't you just love that?

It doesn't matter how dark a region is; the light that is in you is so much greater.

"Greater is He who is in you, than he that is in the world" (1 John 4:4 NIV).

It's irrelevant how spiritually dry a certain location is; the springs of glory and rivers of power that are within you are so much greater.

You might ask, "Well, if so much glory is in me, why don't I see more of it manifesting?" Jesus would say to you, "Did I not say to you that if you believe, you will see the glory of God?" (John 11:40 NASB).

A man who walked in ever-increasing revival was Brother Lawrence – a Christian monk from the 1600s. He wasn't a big-shot preacher, but a dishwasher in the monastery.

He so carried the glory, that people came from all around to just watch him wash dishes, because his face would glow with heavenly peace and joy!

He never labored for the glory, but instead just simply turned his attention and affections to the Lord; and as he turned to the Lord in simple faith, he wrote that it, "often causes in me joys and great delight inwardly, and sometimes also it manifests itself outwardly. It is so great that I am forced to use means to moderate them and prevent their manifestations to others."[95]

---

[95] Brother Lawrence, *Practicing the Presence of God*, Letter 2

You Are a Walking Revival

Brother Lawrence didn't strive for revival, the only striving he did was to conceal his ridiculous joy, because people couldn't handle it!

In one of his letters, he wrote, "When I apply myself to prayer I feel all my spirit and all my soul lift itself up into His presence without any care or effort of mine. It continues in this state as though it were suspended and firmly fixed in God as in its center and place of rest."[96]

Again, he didn't stress or strain his way into revival, but with ease, trusted in the Lord and found himself immersed in the glory of God.

Toward the end of his life, he penned, "Let us seek Him often by faith. He is within us. Seek Him not elsewhere."[97]

Brother Lawrence's key to practicing the presence of God was that he had faith in the underground springs – Mr. Revival within. Do you recognize His presence within you?

Flapping or Soaring

You might be saying, "I really want to live in ever-increasing revival; should I be trying harder and harder to make revival happen?" Well, I believe the true breakthrough is in trusting the Lord like Brother Lawrence. The Scriptures tell us, "Oh, the utter extravagance of his work in us who trust him – endless energy, boundless strength!" (Ephesians 1:19 MSG).

The formula for revival is not striving in the flesh, but learning to trust in the promises of God.

The hummingbird knows what it's like to strive in the flesh. Have you seen a hummingbird fly? Their wings beat at a

---
[96] Lawrence, *Practicing the Presence of God*, Letter 2
[97] Lawrence, *Practicing the Presence of God*, Letter 15

hysterical eight to ten beats a second. Hummingbirds also live no longer than three years, and can occasionally end up as snake food because they can't fly at high altitudes.

Now, eagles have a whole different operating system. Eagles know how to do more than flap, they know how to soar! They know how to depend on the strength of the wind.

Eagles live ten times longer than hummingbirds and they eat snakes for breakfast, lunch, and dinner.

The Lord spoke to me through the hummingbird and eagle, that Christians who depend on the power of the flesh will burn out in a couple of years, and they will be devoured by the enemy.

But, the Christian who has learned to trust in the Lord and His great and precious promises, will soar from glory to glory, will have longevity in revival, and will destroy the works of the devil!

Abraham's Revival

God promised to make Abraham the father of many nations, and how Abraham longed for it! But there was a problem: his wife Sarah was barren!

Abraham was at a fork in the road. He had the promise before him, as well as the problem. As they focused on the problem, fear filled their heart. Fear will always put you in the flesh, or human striving.

So, he and Sarah decided that they would have Abraham procreate with their slave-girl, Hagar. Abraham jumped into the tent with Hagar, and nine-months later, Ishmael was born. Ishmael was the product of Abraham's human efforts and wisdom, and therefore, he wasn't God's perfect will.

Ishmael is a picture of imitation revival.

However, the time soon came when both Abraham and Sarah were beyond child-bearing years. It was then that Abraham finally came to the end of himself. Faith begins when self-trust ends.

Now, all Abraham could do was trust in the promises of God. Sure enough, as he did, that's when the supernatural power of God invaded Abraham's life!

Abe had a physical revival (if you know what I mean), and so did Sarah! He started feeling supernatural power surge through his body, and he looked over at Sarah and asked,

"Are you feeling it, Honey?"

She said, "I sure am, you're the hottest hundred year old man I've ever seen – come here!" They jumped in the tent, had their fireworks show, and nine-months later ... Isaac was born!

Isaac was the product of simple, absolute trust in God's Word. Isaac is a picture of true revival!

It's worth mentioning that after Isaac, Abraham went on to have more children – talk about an ever-increasing revival!

You cannot manufacture revival by human effort or wisdom; you can only receive it when you come to the end of your efforts and start to trust in the promises of God!

What do you do when you have a promise from God, but you also have a problem sticking out its ugly face?

Learn from the story of Abraham.

If you focus on the problem, you will open the door to fear, and you will be walking in the flesh and missing God's perfect will for your life!

But, when you focus on the promises of God's Word, you will open to the door to faith, and you will walk in the power of the Holy Spirit right into God's perfect will!

NEVER BURN OUT: Discover the Reality of your Identity

I'm not saying you deny the problems, but by focusing on the promises of God you will defy the problems!

Focus on the Problem	Focus on the Promises of God
Invites FEAR	Invites FAITH
Fear will put you in the FLESH	Faith will put you in the SPIRIT
You will make MISTAKES	You will fulfill the PERFECT WILL OF GOD
Counterfeit Revival	Real Revival

Moses the Revivalist

Moses was a true revivalist, wasn't he?

Think about what happened through Moses' life: Israel got born-again (in a way); they got free from slavery and oppression which had lasted four-hundred long years (longer than the history of the United States)! In revival, Satan's captives are set free, social justice is served, and precious people are delivered from problems that have plagued their family-trees for hundreds of years. I think we would all like to be used to deliver people out of bondage. The question is, "How do we become that revivalist?"

When Moses was the prince of Egypt, he witnessed an Egyptian beating the daylights out of an Israelite, and he jumped in and killed the Egyptian. When he knew that the word had gotten out, he ran for his life from Pharaoh, and ended up in the backside of the desert for 40 years. Moses had the calling of a revivalist on his life, even when he was a prince in Egypt, but his flesh definitely got in the way!

You Are a Walking Revival

Every Christian has a legitimate calling to be a revivalist, but when we try to bring revival by trusting in our own human efforts and ideas, we will fail.

When Moses tried to bring revival to the children of Israel, while trusting in his own power, he messed everything up and ended up in the desert for 40 years. But that is also where he came to the end of himself, realizing that he just couldn't do it. And that's when God found Moses ready to embark on the journey of faith to deliver the Israelites. That's also when Moses was divinely enabled to live out his great calling and destiny!

Faith begins when self-trust ends.

Just like Abraham and Moses, we must realize that we can't bring true revival by trying harder or with more self-effort, but only by trusting in the promises of God by faith.

Plug Your Faith into the Right Socket

"You foolish Galatians! Who has bewitched you? Before your very eyes Jesus Christ was clearly portrayed as crucified. I would like to learn just one thing from you: Did you receive the Spirit by observing the law, or by believing what you heard? Are you so foolish? After beginning with the Spirit, are you now trying to attain your goal by human effort? ... Does God give you his Spirit and work miracles among you because you observe the law, or because you believe what you heard?" (Galatians 3:1-3 & 5 NIV).

Even today, like the Galatians, some Christians think that it's only through their perfect law-keeping performance that they will earn the right to experience Mr. Revival! They think they need to perfectly perform their way to be merited a Revivalist Badge. The truth is that on the cross Jesus qualified you to experience Mr. Revival and be a revivalist. If you want to do something great for God, first be grounded in what He's already done for you!

There is nothing wrong with wanting revival. But, there is something wrong when you are contending for revival while your "truster" is plugged into the socket of your measly human efforts and your list of good works. Not much power will come out of plugging into that circuit. Plug your "truster" in the socket of God's grace, the finished work of the cross, the great promises of God's Word, and see what happens.

Certainly obeying the commandments of God are extremely important; however, trusting in your good works couldn't get you saved, and still can't make you a revivalist.

The ever-increasing revival has already been given to you by God's grace as a gift. Have you unwrapped it by faith? Or, are you still trying to pay for the gift?

During the revival that broke out under Philip's ministry in the book of Acts, Simon the Sorcerer got baptized. He was the witch – who switched! He clearly saw the power of God was greater than any kind of witchcraft. One day, Simon saw Peter and John in action. They were laying hands on people, imparting revival fire. Amazed, Simon too wanted to be a revivalist. So, he offered money to the Apostles for it. Simon was heavily rebuked for thinking such a thing – and Peter bluntly told him, "May your money perish with you, because you thought you could buy the gift of God with money! You have no part or share in this ministry, because your heart is not right before God" (Acts 8:20-21 NIV).

Today, we might not depend on our debit cards to become revivalists, but if we depend on our fleshly strivings and brownie-point percentage, rather than the promises of God and Christ's finished work, we might just end up in the same boat of foolishness as Simon; having no part or share in ever-increasing revival.

Toiling or Harvesting?

During my college years, I fasted 250 days over a two year period, prayed about six hours a day, slept only four to five hours each night, spent much time doing street outreaches, and sacrificed a social life – in hopes for revival.

But, I didn't really understand and believe the great promises from God's Word which I am sharing throughout this book, so I came out empty.

I had zeal! But I didn't know or believe in the reality of my new identity in Christ. Zeal without knowledge or revelation does not accomplish too much. Paul wrote of the religious Jews saying, "For I can testify about them that they are zealous for God, but their zeal is not based on knowledge" (Romans 10:2 NIV). As humans we are easily impressed by a person's zeal. However, zeal doesn't impress God, nor release God's power. Only faith does. Faith is not the absence of knowledge, but is based on the knowledge of God's Word.

Zeal - Knowledge of God's Word = Religious Striving

Zeal + Knowledge of God's Word = Faith

The disciples fished all night and came out empty every time they dropped their nets. Discouraged they were. Then, they came to the end of themselves.

That's when Jesus spoke a word over them, declaring, "'Throw your net on the right side of the boat and you will find some.' When they did, they were unable to haul the net in because of the large number of fish" (John 21:6 NIV).

OK, so what made the difference?

All night they were fishing without revelation; without a promise from God. But when Jesus spoke "you will find some," they now had a promise from God, and when they fished from the promise – they got a supernatural harvest! Fishing or contending without a promise is called striving in the flesh. Striving in the flesh is not the key to revival.

When you fish for revival as one possessed by the promises of God, you will see a harvest! Here are three promises that we don't fish for, but fish from:

1. God's will for our lives is ever-increasing revival!
2. The price for revival has been paid by Jesus on the cross![98]
3. You are a walking revival because Mr. Revival (the Holy Spirit) is living in you!

Please don't think I'm promoting laziness. The disciples did obey Jesus and lower their nets, right? That's important to factor in. Some Christians are horrible stewards of their time and talents and throw excellent living and obedience to God out the window in the name of "trusting in the promises of God." That's foolish.

We must be passionate about revival, faithful to our calling, live by God's standards, and be obedient to the Holy Spirit's leading. But, we aren't called to do these things divorced from the promises of God! Rather, your obedience and service to God ought to be drenched and dripping in His wonderful promises!

Refuse to Settle for Presence-less, Power-less Christianity

We had just arrived at a church in Haiti.

This church building was nothing more than a tent flapping

---

[98] Christians who think that they need to pay the price for revival, don't understand how great the price is – they'd have to pay for the sins of the world! We couldn't do it, so Jesus did it for us!

with the breeze, but it was packed with hundreds of Haitians – some were born-again, some weren't. I was getting ready to preach the gospel to those precious people who had recently suffered from the tragic 7.0 earthquake.

Before I was invited to take the pulpit, I heard the Holy Spirit speak to me, "Start the meeting by calling up the blind and everyone with eye problems, and you and the team will lay hands on them and see them healed. Then, you can preach." That word from the Lord made me a little nervous at first. "What if nothing happens? They will not listen to my preaching if I call up the blind and nobody gets healed," I thought.

I knew I had a choice. I could either settle for powerless Christianity that is all talk without any demonstration ... or, I could just go for it! I went for it!

We called them up to the front and about a dozen people walked forward, facing the crowd. One by one, we laid hands on them, and eyes were healed. A number of them gave powerful testimonies.

One man told the crowd that as soon as we laid hands on his eyes, a hot liquid fell from his eyes, and now his vision was clear! We had such a glorious service. They paid close attention to everything that I preached, and the presence of God came in a powerful way.

Toward the end of the meeting, the presence of the Lord was very thick. Many Haitians were healed of all sorts of conditions. The pastor's wife even testified of her handicapped legs being restored. Our hearts were all touched by the love of God. The gospel went forth with power and glory.

Imagine what can and will happen when we refuse to settle for powerless, presence-less Christianity?

NEVER BURN OUT: Discover the Reality of your Identity

As crazy as it sounds, not everybody desires revival. Some would rather settle for having a form of Christianity that denies the power of God. Some would settle for head-knowledge rather than the glory of God. Others are just content with having their cute church services and programs. Others think that revival is nothing more than church growth. Many are just fine with playing church.

Playing church without the glory of God is like playing a guitar without strings – pointless.

"The only reason we don't have revival is we are willing to live without it!"[99] – Leonard Ravenhill

How much do you desire revival? Yes, God desires ever-increasing revival for us. Yes, the price for revival has been paid. Yes, Mr. Revival is living in us. But the question still remains, "Do you desire it?"

God's promises telling us that we are walking revivals were given to inject us with a surge of holy passion; they aren't sleeping pills.

The enemy would love to see the church be overcome by a passivity spirit, and not have a burning desire to see the Kingdom of God manifest on this earth in greater dimensions.

Once the Lord spoke to me saying, "passivity precedes slumber!" Some of God's people are in spiritual slumber, where they are sleep-walking through the motions of church, but they are not even aware that they've been tranquilized by the enemy, who has them exactly where he wants them.

If that's you, the Lord would say to you, "Wake up!" (Revelation 3:2) and "Be zealous" (Revelation 3:19). You have no time to be spiritually sleeping; you are a walking revival!

---

[99] http://www.leonard-ravenhill.com/quotes

Chapter 9

You Are Adopted!

Michael Jordan was rejected from making his high school basketball team when he was a sophomore. At this date, he has been chosen as the NBA's Most Valuable Player five times. He has won six championships and has two Olympic Gold Medals. Do you think he's still crying about his high school rejection?

When Beyonce Knowles auditioned for Star Search, which was the biggest talent show on national TV at the time, she was rejected. But after winning sixteen Grammys, including a record-breaking six awards in one night, I'm sure she's gotten over her Star Search rejection by now.

Child of God, have you gotten over your past rejections?

Yes, people might have rejected us in times past, but that is absolutely nothing compared to being adopted by our Father.

Being adopted by God Himself is more valuable than anything in this world. We no longer need to be living in the pain of past rejections. We've been given the promotion of all promotions. We've won the prize of all prizes. We have received the highest honor available to humanity!

Just as light is the opposite of darkness, adoption is the opposite of rejection. When you flip on the lights, darkness has to leave. In the same way, when you were adopted, rejection was expelled. You have been adopted. Therefore, you are not a reject!

> "So you have not received a spirit that makes you fearful slaves. Instead, you received God's Spirit when he adopted you as his own children. Now we call him, 'Abba, Father'" (Romans 8:15: NLT).

Our adoption process started at the cross:

> "Then at three o'clock Jesus called out with a loud voice, 'Eloi, Eloi, lema sabachthani?' which means 'My God, my God, why have you abandoned me?'" (Mark 15:34 NLT).

What's strange about this verse is that as Jesus was hanging on the bloody cross, He referred to His Father as "My God," not "My Father." Clearly, Jesus proudly addressed God as His father throughout His life on earth. Jesus always prayed addressing Him as Father, and even encouraged His disciples to do likewise. You see, the significance is that on the cross, Jesus became an orphan. Why? So we could forever be God's adopted children!

The cross is the greatest import and export center of the ages. Jesus imported our orphan spirit and all of our rejection issues, and exported to us sonship and the spirit of adoption.

You Are Adopted

It is evident from the teaching of the Scriptures that not every human being on the face of the earth is a child of God. In fact, Jesus called the self-righteous Pharisees children of the devil.[100]

How does one receive this gift of adoption? It's only through receiving Jesus Christ by faith.

"But to all who did receive him, who believed in his name, he gave the right to become children of God" (John 1:12 NIV).

What Kind of Father Is God?

1. God Is a Loving Father

Do you want to know how much He loves you? He loves you as much as He loves Jesus![101] Can you believe it?

> *Being adopted by God Himself is more valuable than anything in this world.*

Use your imagination and picture the Holy Father looking at His perfect Son Jesus. What is the expression on the Father's face? Love. Joy. Acceptance. Delight. Now, use your imagination to picture the Father's face as He is looking directly at you; what's on His face? Disgust? Hate? Bitterness? No.

The same love-based emotions that the Father has toward Jesus are the very emotions that He feels toward us.

2. God Is a Perfect Father

Jesus knew very well that our earthly fathers would be far from perfect, so He compared and contrasted your earthly father with your Heavenly Father:

---
[100] See John 8:44
[101] See John 17:13

"If you, then, though you are evil, know how to give good gifts to your children, how much more will your Father in heaven give good gifts to those who ask him!" (Matthew 7:11 NIV).

Jesus was essentially saying, "Your earthly fathers are far from perfect in their fathering, and some of them can still do an OK job! ... but your heavenly Father is on a whole different level; He's a perfect Father!"

3. God Is a Good Father

Jesus knew the Father better than anybody. He revealed to us that our Father is good. Do you really believe in the goodness of your heavenly Father? If you doubt His goodness, you will face problems throughout life.

Remember the story of the prodigal son?[102]

The younger son pulls from his inheritance, which was a slap in the face to his father, then the punk ventured off to tackle sin mountain. Sin mountain did what it does best, it chewed him up and spit him out.

The boy finally came to his senses, and decided to go home and beg his dad for a job. He had already given up on his sonship. To his astonishment, as he was returning home, he saw his father had been waiting for his return all along. The father was overjoyed at the return of his son. He embraced his son, clothed him, and threw him a party. This is the heart of our Father in heaven.

He desires to embrace us, cover our sin and shame, and throw a Holy Ghost party for all of His children! The Holy Ghost party is ever-increasing revival.

---
[102] See Luke 15:11-31

You Are Adopted

Well, this masterful story takes an interesting spin when the older brother hears the music from the party and realizes that his father has killed the best cow for his naughty brother, and the older brother gets jealously ticked.

By the way, when your brother or sister in Christ gets blessed by the Father, you can either hate or participate.

The gracious father came out to see his older son, and the older son vents his fury and frustration saying:

> *When your brother or sister gets blessed by the Father, you can either hate or participate.*

"All these years I've slaved for you and never once refused to do a single thing you told me to. And in all that time you never gave me even one young goat for a feast with my friends. Yet when this son of yours comes back after squandering your money on prostitutes, you celebrate by killing the fattened calf!" (Luke 15:29-30 NLT).

Obviously, the older son had a jealousy issue.

Whenever we underestimate the goodness of our Father, that's exactly when jealousy infests our lives.

The father's response to his jealous son is classic: "Look, dear son, you have always stayed by me, and everything I have is yours" (Luke 15:31 NLT).

Did you get that?

There was no need for the older son to be jealous over his brother's party, because everything the father had belonged to the older son. He could have had a party anytime, he just needed to ask. Perhaps the older son never did, because he doubted the goodness of his father.

The older brother typifies many Christians who underestimate the goodness of their Father, and so they have the prayer lives of a bastard. If the older brother had understood the goodness of his father, his brother's party would have excited him. He would've thought to himself, "Wow, if Dad can do that for him, he can also do it for me. How exciting!"

When I see my brothers and sisters get blessed, I get pumped up, because I just saw what is on my Daddy's blessing menu. So I can ask Him for the same blessing. When I was single, I heard many men of God brag about how God gave them the greatest wife in the world. I didn't pout or host a pity-party saying, "Why am I still single?" No. I went to prayer, and believed God for an excellent wife, and wow, did the Lord bless me!

There would be less jealousy in the body of Christ and more Holy Ghost parties, if we just got the revelation of the goodness of our Father.

Have you been the jealous older brother? Have you underestimated the goodness of your Father? It's time to get free of all that junk.

4. God Is an Adoptive Father

God is our adoptive Father. But don't get me wrong, we still have been born of God, and we have His DNA coursing through our being (as we saw in Chapter 2). Yet, the Scriptures reveal to us that God is also our adoptive Father, and this is significant.

You Are Adopted

The very fact that God adopted us tells us that we were originally born to a different father. In fact, we were born as children of the devil.[103]

We were born with a fallen nature. We "were by nature children of wrath, like the rest of mankind" (Ephesians 2:3b NIV). However, thanks be to God who rescued us.

The truth that we have been adopted communicates to us that we have been chosen. While not every child-birth may have been the perfect will of the parents,[104] every adoption is the perfect will of the adoptive parents.

A famous movie star had a son with major birth defects. This movie star is known to be a true tough guy, but he did a wimpy thing and gave his own son up for adoption because He didn't want to deal with the challenges. The baby was tossed around different foster homes, then, finally, a precious couple decided to adopt that boy. They knew about his needy condition and the implications of it, but still wanted him.

> *God knew everything about me and you. He knew that we were capable of grieving Him. Yet, He still went out of His way to adopt us because He wanted us so much.*

God knows everything about me and you. He knew that we were extremely needy. He knew that we were capable of grieving Him. Yet, He still went out of His way to adopt us because He wanted us that much.

---

[103] See 1 John 3:10
[104] (although every baby is the perfect will of God)

"For he chose us in him before the creation of the world to be holy and blameless in his sight. In love he predestined us to be adopted as his sons through Jesus Christ, in accordance with his pleasure and will – " (Ephesians 1:4-5 NIV).

Before the foundations of the world, He chose to adopt us. Why, you ask?

Adopting you and me brought Him so much pleasure! It's only when we are convinced that God takes full pleasure in us, that we can start taking full pleasure in Him. God finds immense pleasure in you, not because of what you've done for Him, but because of who you are to Him.

Who Chose Who?

I remember riding in a car with some friends, and we spent a good hour or two of our road trip discussing this question: "Did I choose God, or did God choose me?"

Half of them thought they were the ones who actually chose God, and the other half of us believed that it was God who chose us.

The half that believed they chose God concluded this because they had been seriously searching for God for a long time. The other half that concluded that God chose them were those who weren't even seeking God, but had been ambushed by a powerful encounter with the Lord.

However, our opinions don't matter too much, in light of what the Scriptures tell us. The Scriptures teach us that ultimately, God chose us before history even began.

You Are Adopted

"Even before he made the world, God loved us and chose us in Christ to be holy and without fault in his eyes" (Ephesians 1:4 NLT).

It doesn't matter if you were on a forty-day fast, crying out at the top of your lungs for Jesus to reveal Himself to you, or if you were blindsided like the Apostle Paul. The underlying truth is that God chose you before the world was made.

Do you see the whole picture? To say that we were the ones who really chose God is not seeing the full picture – the whole truth. If knowing the truth sets us free,[105] knowing the full truth will bring us full freedom from pride, and full freedom into God's grace. The full truth is not that we chose God, but that He chose us.

> *It's only when we are convinced that God takes full pleasure in us, that we can start taking full pleasure in Him.*

The disciples James and John, too, could have claimed to have chosen Jesus. In fact, when they heard Jesus calling them, they left their father and their family fishing business to follow the Rabbi.

Matthew left his life in tax-collecting because he chose to be a disciple of Jesus. Peter left everything to follow Jesus and serve Him.

But, Jesus makes it clear to all of them, "You did not choose me, but I chose you" (John 15:16a ESV).

Like James, John, Matthew, and Peter, you may be serving the Lord wholeheartedly, and have given up much for the sake of Christ, but the fact of the matter is: God chose you first!

[105] See John 8:32

NEVER BURN OUT: Discover the Reality of your Identity

Vending Machine Christianity

Is this how you view your relationship with God?

1. "If I do good to God, then God will do good to me."
2. "If I give to God, God will give to me."
3. "If I honor God, then God will honor me."
4. "If I chose God, then God will choose me."

Now, there are some truths in these statements. The Scriptures teach on sowing and reaping. God told Samuel that He will honor those who honor Him. The Lord tells us that we can't serve two masters, and calls us to choose Him. But, all this is not the full truth about your relationship with God.

Jesus said, "You shall know the truth, and the truth shall set you free" (John 8:32). Did you know that if we only see partial truth, we will only walk in partial freedom ... from pride?

Those who think the Christian life is all about "me initiating and God responding" are short-sighted, pride-prone, stressed out individuals, who will have a hard time sustaining ever-increasing revival.

What's the full truth then?

Here it is...

1. God has been so good to us, that we want to do good works for God, and God promises to reward us for what we've gladly done.
2. God gave to us more than we know, and out of gratitude we get to cheerfully give to Him; as we do, there is a sowing and reaping effect that takes place!

3. God first honored us with the greatest honor in the universe – to be His children; and because God's grace changed our hearts, now we want to honor the Lord with everything in us. As we do, the Lord honors us for honoring Him.

4. God first chose us, so we were able to choose Him, and as we chose Him, He chose us.

What I'm trying to say is that everything starts and ends with God. He is the "Alpha and Omega" (Revelation 1:8 NIV), I'm not the Alpha and He the Omega.

He is the "author and finisher of our faith" (Hebrews 12:2 KJV); the author desires the glory for His masterpiece!

Paul writes, "Who has first given God anything, so as to receive payment in return?" (Romans 11:35 Weymouth).

> *Christianity is not a vending machine, where you put in three quarters and get a prize. Christianity is a joyful response to God's grace!*

Christianity is not a vending machine, where you put in your three quarters and get a prize! Instead, Christianity is a joyful response to God's grace!

We need to embrace each aspect:

- **First step:** God's grace – "What God has done."
- **Second step**: Your response – "What we do."
- **Third step:** God's reward – "What God will do."

Do you see the full picture? Or, do you only see Step 2 and Step 3? If you only understand steps 2 and 3, you will go through the joyless motions of a malfunctioning Christianity – which will burn out sooner or later!

On the other hand, when you really see Step 1, which shows the grace of God; when you step out to do Step 2, the power of God will invade your life as winds behind your sails! When the strong winds are propelling you, you will experience acceleration in your spiritual growth! Remember, strong winds behind a baseball turn an "out" into a "home run!"

Are you seeing that the full story of our salvation doesn't start with us choosing God out of our free will, but God choosing us by His grace?

He is the author of our eternal salvation.[106] God started and finished the epic story of my salvation. Because it's His story, He rightfully deserves the glory.

"But you are a chosen people" (1 Peter 2:9a NIV).

"Who shall bring any charge against God's elect?" (Romans 8:3a ESV).

The Importance of Knowing You Are Chosen

As believers, knowing that we are chosen by God is not to make us doubt His goodness toward un-believers, but to make us soak in His goodness toward us.

The reason why Christians are told that we are chosen, is so that we will not be puffed up in pride, but rather remain humble. Nothing is more humbling than the unearned grace of God.

---
[106] See Hebrews 5:9

You Are Adopted

Throughout my life, I was deeply interested in studying the lives of men and women who were used by God to change the world. I studied to see if I could learn the secrets to their success.

I remember reading an interview done with a man of God from an Asian country who was very instrumental in bringing the Gospel to his entire continent. When he was asked to share the keys to his fruitful ministry, he responded, "I pray and I obey." I remember those five words piercing me to my core. I stood in such awe of this man's discipline and passion. I really honor him for making such great decisions.

A few years later, I stumbled upon a study of the life of another man of God from the U.S. who was used by God to revolutionize the body of Christ. He was asked a similar question, but the way he responded was a bit strange to me at first.

He said, "It is not because I pray more than other men, or made all the right decisions. I've made many mistakes, but it's purely the grace of God that He chose me." When I heard that, I stood in awe of God's grace.

The first man of God magnified the choices that he had made. The second, magnified the choice that God made.

I'm not discounting the importance of making wise choices – we all know that's important. But, at the end of the day, I don't want to boast in my choices, but His choice!

> "Let him who boasts, boast in the Lord."
> - the Apostle Paul

Sharing about the wise choices you've made can be very helpful to others. Ultimately, we boast in the grace of God and we must declare, like Paul, "By the grace of God I am what I am" (1 Corinthians 15:10a ESV).

Why did God choose to adopt you and me? Do not come up with your own reasons why He chose you, such as: it was because we fervently sought after Him, or we had a generous heart, or even had a thousand people praying for us.

> *Ultimately, we boast in the grace of God and we must declare, like Paul, "By the grace of God I am what I am."*

You might have had all those things going for you, or you might have had none of those things going for you; it's all irrelevant, because the reason God chose us is His great love for us.

"We know, dear brothers and sisters, that God loves you and has chosen you to be his own people" (1 Thessalonians 1:4 NLT).

You see, it wasn't your noble choosing of God that caused God to want to repay you by choosing you.

Again, God is not a vending machine. The whole story, the full truth, is that even before we chose Him, He chose us. While we deserved nothing more than to be eternal cast-aways, our God chose us to eternally be His children!

Our Heavenly Father's Mission Statement

Most successful companies and churches have a Mission Statement. A Mission Statement might only be one or two sentences, but it will accurately capture and convey the heart of the organization. What's God's mission statement when it comes to fathering us?

Recently, I was having lunch with my friend Leo who, with his wife Terry, had adopted a young teenage girl a few years ago. I asked Leo, "What have you learned about the heart of our Heavenly Father toward His children?" I assumed that He had much revelation regarding our adoption as children of God.

I was so blown away at what came out of his mouth. He told me that before they took in their adoptive daughter, God spoke to him, saying, "There are only two things that I want you to accomplish with your daughter: These two things are the most important. If you can successfully get these two things done, everything else will fall into place."

The Lord went on to tell him what those two things were: "First, teach her how to receive love ... and second, teach her how to give love away (this will be a by-product of the first)."

As he relayed to me what the Lord had spoken to him, tears welled up in his eyes, and I felt chills race down my spine as I felt the love of our Heavenly Father in such a tangible way. I began to see it more clearly than ever.

What is the mission statement of God in His fathering relationship to us? Is it, "Teach my kids how to never tick me off"? Is it, "Get my kids to work their butts off to make me proud"? I doubt it.

I dare to propose that the Mission Statement of our Heavenly Father is to first teach us how to receive love, and then to give that love away. Why? Because in His infinite wisdom, He knows that if we can be successful in those things, everything else will take care of itself.

NEVER BURN OUT: Discover the Reality of your Identity

You see, when we truly receive God's love, the Bible says that we will then be able to love God and other people. "We love because He first loved us."[107]

When you know you are freely loved, and you learn to freely give that love away, in that process you are automatically keeping all God's commandments.[108] All the commandments are summed up in love: "The entire law is summed up in a single command: Love your neighbor as yourself" (Galatians 5:14 NIV).

Did you notice that we love others "as ourselves"? Did you know that we can also reject others "as ourselves"? In the same way you reject yourself, you will reject others. So, did you know you can hate others or condemn others "as ourselves"?

> Many people do not know how to love others in a healthy way, because they do not love themselves in a healthy way.

You see, the way that you see yourself is quite often how you see others. This is why so many people do not know how to love others in a healthy way, because they do not first know how to love themselves in a healthy way.

What does it mean to love yourself in a healthy way? It means to see yourself as a loved person.

One day, a well-known pastor walked up to me. As I looked up at him, he told me candidly, "I see the hand of God on your life, and the Lord's anointing has always been on you, but you need to let the Lord FATHER YOU!"

[107] See 1 John 4:19
[108] See Romans 13:9

You Are Adopted

When he said that, I felt a witness in my spirit, but I didn't have a clue what that meant.

However, when I heard from Leo over lunch about what the Lord had told him about how to father his adopted daughter, the dots connected, and I received a revelation of what it means to let God father me.

Are you letting the Lord father you? Our Father has been doing all He can to teach us how much He loves us.

1. He gave us His Son. Jesus Christ is the most powerful picture of how much the Father loves us.

2. He led His Son to die on the cross. The cross is the most powerful demonstration of how much God loves us. The Scriptures tell us, "God demonstrates His own love for us in that while we were yet sinners, Christ died for us" (Romans 5:8).

3. He gave us the gospel. The gospel that we are to preach to the ends of the earth is essentially a message about God's love.

4. He sent the Holy Spirit to us. In this era, the Holy Spirit is on a mission to pour the love of God into our hearts,[109] so we would know the Father's love.

Do you get it? That Father has been trying to teach us how to receive His love. He's been trying to get us to see ourselves as lovable people. That's the first part of His mission.

Secondly, He is on a mission to teach us how to give that love away. We must understand that the commandments in the Scriptures were not given to us as:

---
[109] See Romans 5:5

NEVER BURN OUT: Discover the Reality of your Identity

"101 ways to get God to love you"

"Directions on how to get God's affections"

"A manual on how to win God over"

No!

The commandments of Scripture were written to God's covenant people who are already loved.

You see, the commandments of Scripture were given so that we would get a practical understanding of what life looks like for a person who receives God's love and learns to give it away.

"The entire law is summed up in a single command: Love your neighbor as yourself" (Galatians 5:14 NIV).

Do you really want to know what your Father in heaven wants from you? He wants you to live like a loved person.

Chapter 10

You Are His Bride

When I was nineteen years old, I was praying extensively one Saturday night when I fell into a trance. In this powerful experience, I saw a dark bedroom and a beautiful woman dressed in white was just about to climb into bed with a hideous creature. Then I heard the voice of the Lord speaking crystal clearly into my spirit saying, "Bring My people back to Me, bring My people back to Me, bring My people back to Me!" I broke into tears as I felt the heart of God for His people who were so beautiful to Him and clothed in His priceless righteousness. But they were flirting with the devil and he was luring them into the bed of deception, compromise, and sin.

Up until the time I had this unforgettable encounter with the Lord, I had never heard a sermon or teaching on how we are the Bride of Christ. But the Lord gave me a first-hand revelation on how He literally yearns for our wholehearted love.

NEVER BURN OUT: Discover the Reality of your Identity

Father Abraham sent his bondservant to find a bride for His beloved son Isaac.[110] This is a powerful picture of our Father in heaven, sending the Holy Spirit to woo a bride for Jesus the Son. The Holy Spirit is in the business of wooing us to Jesus the Bridegroom.

As you read this chapter, may you receive a first-hand understanding that we are the Bride of Christ – the object of the Bridegroom's deep affections.

He Likes Us

Jesus' heart doesn't burn with desire for us because of our works, but because of His grace. Therefore, I can't tell you why He desires us so much. Works are explainable. Grace isn't.

We were the "joy set before" Jesus, that gave Him the strength He needed to endure the cross.[111] His heart toward us has not changed. We never deserved to be the joy of His heart in the first place. You can't earn it; you can only accept it. If you are trying to earn it, you cannot reciprocate it. If you humbly accept it, you can't help but reciprocate it.

"We love because He first loved us."[112]

Does Jesus our Bridegroom love us, like us, or both? Both. For Him, to love you doesn't mean He likes you. What's the difference?

To love somebody means you forgive and bless them. To like somebody means that you enjoy them. Big difference.

We are commanded to love everyone, but we are not commanded to like everyone. Thank God! You have to love your enemies, but you don't have to enjoy them.

---
[110] See Genesis 24
[111] See Hebrews 12:2
[112] See 1 John 4:19

You Are His Bride

Jesus doesn't just tolerate us in love. He enjoys us. He cherishes us.[113] As I just mentioned, we were the "joy set before Him" (Hebrews 12:2) two-thousand years ago, as He walked the hill of Calvary. And, we still are.

Contrary to Dan Brown's *The Da Vinci Code*, while Jesus was on earth, He never had a wife. He was saving all of His affections for His Bride – us.

Jesus was crucified during the Jewish feast of Passover. In fact, Passover was just a type and foreshadow of the cross of Christ. Passover was a special time when the entire Song of Songs was read as liturgy.[114] The Song of Songs is a love story between a king and his bride. It is an Old Testament picture that sheds insight into the New Testament principle of our relationship with Jesus the Bridegroom. The early church saw the Song of Songs as a secret message that revealed Jesus' love for the Church.[115]

As Jesus took up the cross, He was mesmerized by His bride. I'm convinced that as He thought about us, He mentally rehearsed these verses from the Song of Songs that had just been recited over Passover:

> "You have captivated my heart, my sister, my bride; you have captivated my heart with one glance of your eyes, with one jewel of your necklace. How beautiful is your love, my sister, my bride! How much better is your love than wine, and the fragrance of your oils than any spice!" (Song of Songs 4:9-10 ESV).

We were the joy set before Him. And, guess what? He still likes us.

---

[113] See Ephesians 5:28-32
[114] Jewish Study Bible, p. 1566
[115] John Michael Talbot, The *Lover and the Beloved*, p 7

NEVER BURN OUT: Discover the Reality of your Identity

Why We Must Get This!

"Husbands should love their wives as their own bodies. He who loves his wife loves himself. For no one ever hated his own flesh, but nourishes and cherishes it, just as Christ does the church, because we are members of his body. 'Therefore a man shall leave his father and mother and hold fast to his wife, and the two shall become one flesh.' This mystery is profound, and I am saying that it refers to Christ and the church" (Ephesians 5:28-32 ESV).

Some men might be irritated by the fact that they are the Bride of Christ. But every man and woman needs this revelation. It's perverted thinking and insecurity in our masculinity that causes us men to get offended at this spiritual reality. Coming to know Jesus as the Bridegroom will only make us into better husbands and less prone to the deceptive seductions of sexual immorality, as He becomes our fascination. For single women, coming to know Jesus as your Bridegroom will enable you to discern the right man for your life – a man who truly nourishes and cherishes you. For all men and women, coming to know Jesus as your Bridegroom will liberate you from fleshly fantasizing and dangerous daydreaming, as Jesus becomes more than enough for you.

Without knowing Jesus as our Bridegroom, our relationship with God will be incomplete, and our spiritual growth will be stunted.

Sadly, many Christians will travel through their life on earth without thinking much of the fact that we are the Bride of Christ. This is tragic because it will put a ceiling on their intimacy with the Lord. You see, understanding we are the Bride of Christ has the potential to impassion your heart for Jesus like nothing else.

You Are His Bride

Seeing Jesus as the passionate Bridegroom, who always desires His Bride, awakens our desire for Him.

Everybody has a desire to be desired. We naturally shy away from the environments where we don't feel wanted, and gravitate toward the places we feel most desired. The more you see how much Jesus desires you, the more you will be drawn to Him. You will be sucked into His presence, and you may never find your way out!

We live in a world of romance. Yes, because of sin entering into the world, romance has been contaminated on so many levels. Yet, the innate desire to be crazy about someone, and having someone reciprocate that desire, is embedded into humanity. A huge percentage of movies have a romantic storyline. Most of the music albums have a romantic theme.

> *Seeing Jesus as the passionate Bridegroom, who always desires His Bride, awakens our desire for Him.*

As we desire food in the natural, our spirits desire every word that proceeds from the mouth of God. As we desire water in the natural, our spirits desire the presence of the Holy Spirit – who is living water. And, just as we desire romance in the natural, our spirits desire Jesus the Bridegroom.

Worldly romance can and often will blind you and disappoint you. It makes you oblivious to another person's flaws, until those flaws start clawing away at your sanity. Contrarily, romance with Jesus will open your eyes to see how flawless and beautiful He is, and His goodness will only make your life all the more enjoyable.

NEVER BURN OUT: Discover the Reality of your Identity

Romance with Jesus is not sexual, it's spiritual. We have a body, but we are a spirit. Thus, physical union can never satisfy you the way spiritual union with Jesus can. Many people think that physical romance is the epitome of romance, but that's saying that having somebody being romantic with your house is the highest form of romance. Your body is your house.

A reason why so many Christians are getting caught in the web of sexual sin is because they are not enjoying their spiritual union with Jesus. They don't know that Jesus is a passionate Bridegroom who has burning desires for us. They are trying to satisfy a spiritual desire through mere physical means.

When we see Jesus as the lover of our souls, it makes so much sense to want to spend all day with Him, just worshipping.

> "In the Hebrew Old Testament, the primary word for worship means 'to bow down in reverence and submission.' And in the New Testament, the most common Greek word for worship means 'to come forward to kiss.'"[116] – Philip Yancey

In the New Testament, because of who we are in Christ, by grace, and through the cross, our worship is not just an expression of deep reverence for our King (although that is foundational), but fiery passion for our Lover. As we worship, we are kissing the face of our Bridegroom God.

An adopted son might enjoy spending half-an-hour with his dad. A dominion-taking revivalist will not mind spending an hour having a conference call with his Commander-in-Chief. Covenant brothers can enjoy going fishing for half-the-day with each other. But, romantic lovers will spend 24-7 together, and

---

[116] http://www.christianitytoday.com/ct/2005/may/2.80.html?start=2 (Accessed June 10, 2011)

that will still not be enough. When I was dating my wife, I used to purposefully take "long-cuts" after dinner, so I could spend a few more minutes exclusively with her.

Knowing that you are the Bride of Christ will take your worship and prayer life to whole new dimensions. The cap will come off! As you spend time with the Lord, you will think the rapture took place. I'm not kidding. This happened quite often to the Christian mystics who understood that they were the Bride of Christ.

Unlike many men, St. Francis (1182-1226) was very comfortable with his identity as the Bride of Christ. He unashamedly taught this reality to his disciples. As a result, they would lose all track of time in their worship gatherings, hours would go by like minutes, as they were lost in their Bridegroom. One eye witness recorded that, "Francis was often suspended in such sweetness of contemplation that caught up out of himself he could not reveal what he had experienced because it went beyond all human comprehension."[117] Your prayer life can be as such, because you are as much the Bride of Christ as St. Francis.

In her autobiography, Madam Jeanne Guyon (1648-1717) shared how she used to see herself as a "monster of iniquity" who repeatedly misused God's grace time and time again. Then, the Lord started revealing to her through His Word that she was His beloved spouse. This radically transformed everything about her life. She wrote about how this revelation affected her prayer life:

> "Nothing was more easy to me than prayer. Hours passed away like moments, while I could hardly do anything else but pray. The fervency of my love allowed

---
[117] Quoting Celano, found in Talbot, *The Lover and the Beloved*, p. 75

me no intermission. It was a prayer of rejoicing and possessing, devoid of all busy imaginations and forced reflections; it was a prayer of the will, not of the head. The taste of God was so great, so pure, unblended and uninterrupted, and it drew and absorbed the power of my soul ... I had now no sight but Jesus Christ alone."[118]

Even though she was aware of the danger of writing it, she authored a commentary on the Song of Songs, with the point of Jesus being the Bridegroom and the individual believer being the Bride. This book sent her to prison. Today, her books have become well-read Christian classics. Her most well-known and widespread books are on the topic of prayer. This woman had a prayer-life that has been a deep inspiration to believers for hundreds of years. If you want to have that kind of prayer life, you must come to know Jesus as the Bridegroom. You must not see yourself as a "monster of iniquity" but the Bride of Christ!

> *Knowing that you are the Bride of Christ will take your worship and prayer life to whole new dimensions.*

St. Bernard of Clairvaux's (1090-1153) favorite book of the Bible was also the Song of Songs. He taught it extensively from the perspective that we are the Bride of Christ. In his book *Loving God* he passionately explained that just as Solomon's bride didn't understand her value, many Christians don't understand our value as Christ's beautiful Bride, and thus live a bored and inferior life.[119] Do you realize that you are beautiful because you are Christ's Bride?

---
[118] *The Autobiography of Madame Guyon*, Ch. 8
[119] Bernard of Clairvaux, *Loving God*, Ch.2

You Are His Bride

Apparently, St. Bernard got so undone from encountering Jesus through the Song of Songs, that worldly and spiritual entertainment all became boring. He wrote in his commentary on the Song of Songs, "I have no desire for visions and dreams. Clever stories and twists of language, even angelic visitors, bore me. Jesus Himself absolutely outshines them all."[120]

Today, so many Christians are more fascinated with the latest TV series and the newest blockbuster movie than with the Lord. Like St. Bernard, they need to encounter Jesus as the passionate Bridegroom. If angelic visitations got boring to St. Bernard, how much more boring do you think sin became to him?

St. Teresa (1515-1582) knew what it was like to have her affections being torn in two opposite directions, the Lord and the world. But, as she encountered Jesus as the Bridegroom, it was game over. In a vision, Jesus appeared to her, and extended His nail-pierced hand and told her that they nail-pierced His hand so that she would be His promised Bride. He explained that this was not done because she merited it, but it was all because of His grace. He told her that from that day on, she was to honor Him – not just as the Creator, King, and God, but also as her Bridegroom. She wrote about how this experience affected her, "This grace had such an effect on me, that I could not contain myself."[121] She spent the rest of her life as a "pray-er," and much of her life she was literally blissed-out on the person of Jesus. Many times in prayer, her face would begin to visibly glow. One eye-witness records, "On those occasions her face became so radiant, beautiful and devout that one who saw it could never forget it."[122]

---

[120] Cairvaux, *Talks on the Song of Songs*, p. 3
[121] *The Life of St. Teresa of Jesus*, Relation III, pp. 19-20
[122] Fr. Thomas Dubay, *Fire Within*, p.25

NEVER BURN OUT: Discover the Reality of your Identity

By 1990, Mike Bickle knew a whole lot about successful ministry.[123] His church had grown to three-thousand members and he was traveling the world speaking at large conferences. When he was a younger pastor, he had thought that an internationally recognized ministry would bring him satisfaction and excitement. Yet here he was, living his dream, but still feeling bored and empty.

One day as he was reading through the Song of Songs, he had a life-transforming encounter with the passionate heart of his Bridegroom – Jesus Christ. Mike writes, "I felt wooed into a vast ocean of God's burning desire for me. I felt profoundly satisfied as the object of His burning desire."[124] Mike's spiritual life was invigorated as He came to know Jesus as the Bridegroom.

A few years later, his friend called him on the phone and prophesied over him that the Song of Songs would become the focus of his life and ministry for the rest of his life. Mike was a little uncomfortable with this great calling at first, thinking a woman would be a better choice; but he accepted it, and has been used by God to successfully present Jesus as the Bridegroom for the last twenty years. Shortly after, he resigned from the mega-church, and started the International House of Prayer, where 24/7 worship and intercession has taken place for over 10 years.

How do you raise up a company of Christians to worship and pray for 24/7? Teach them that Jesus is the Bridegroom and we are the Bride – the object of His relentless affections.

The Jealousy of the Bridegroom

> "For I am jealous for you with the jealousy of God himself. I promised you as a pure bride to one husband--Christ" (2 Corinthians 11:2 NLT).

---

[123] Story taken from *The Pleasures of Loving God* by Mike Bickle
[124] Bickle, *The Pleasures of Loving God*, p. 10

You Are His Bride

Oprah Winfrey had a problem with God being a jealous God. Her argument was: How can an omnipotent God have such an insecurity issue?

While sinful jealousy is rooted in insecurity, godly jealousy is rooted in total security. God knows who He is, and is confident in what He has to offer.

There is a heaven and hell difference between sinful jealousy and godly jealousy. Those who have been indoctrinated by this world will have a hard time seeing the difference; I trust you will be able to see it.

Sinful jealousy passionately desires what rightfully doesn't belong to them, while godly jealousy passionately desires what does belong to them

Sinful jealousy wants another person's house, car, job, life, looks, spouse, etc. This is a direct violation of the tenth commandment "Thou Shall Not Covet" (Exodus 20:17 KJV).

But godly jealousy wants what is rightfully theirs.

If you are jealous over somebody else's great calling from God, and you constantly daydream about being in their shoes, that's coveting. But, if you are passionate about stepping into everything God has ordained for you to do, that's a healthy form of jealousy, because you are wanting what's rightfully yours.

The best example of godly jealousy would be a husband being jealous for his wife. The writer of Proverbs talks about the wildfire of a husband's jealousy over his wife, and doesn't judge that kind of jealousy as an evil emotion.[125]

This is what Jesus feels toward us. Jesus is not jealous for what does not belong to Him. Do you know why He desires our affections? We belong to Him. We are His Bride.

---
[125] See Proverbs 6:34

God revealed His jealous side only to His covenant people. He was never jealous over the uncircumcised Philistine, or the lewd Babylonian, or the unbeliever, but He is over us – His Bride.

The one thing that makes God jealous is when His people engage in idolatry. When something takes our hearts away from the Lord, that makes Him jealous.

"Do not worship any other god, for the LORD, whose name is Jealous, is a jealous God" (Exodus 34:14 NIV).

"Therefore, my beloved, flee from idolatry ... Or do we provoke the Lord to jealousy? We are not stronger than He, are we?" (1 Corinthians 10:14-22 NIV).

Sinful jealousy is destructive in nature, while godly jealousy is protective in nature

I remember when I was in High School, many of the students who had nice cars had other jealous students scratch their new vehicles using keys. But, godly jealousy is zealous about protecting what somebody else has. When I saw the enemy trying to destroy one of the leaders on my staff, out of jealousy, I did everything I could to stop it.

God's holy jealousy is zealous about protecting your relationship with Him. His jealousy burns hot whenever your intimacy with Him is threatened.

Is there anything in your life that is eating away at your relationship with the passionate Bridegroom? If so, let the fiery love of God for you put that to death.

"For love is as strong as death, its jealousy as enduring as the grave. Love flashes like fire, the brightest kind of flame" (Song of Songs 8:6 NLT).

When the priests of Baal did everything they could to call down fire, and their god didn't respond, they started cutting themselves to get his attention.[126] Cutting themselves was a picture of self-hatred. Idolators will always have their idols eventually fail them, and when that happens, they will start cutting themselves in self-hatred. Never forget, self-hatred is always the product of idolatry. Nothing breaks God's heart like His children living in self-hatred. And that is why God is so protectively jealous for us to be free from idols and to worship only Him; because He knows that only He will never fail us.

Sinful jealousy wants to take from you, while godly jealousy wants to give to you

God longs to give you so much! Therefore, His jealousy burns when anything is keeping you from receiving all He has for you.

Sinful jealousy says, "I'm angry because I want to take what you have, but I can't!" Godly jealousy says, "I'm angry because I want to give you what I have, but I can't!"

If there are two employees trying to hunt down the same promotion, and only one of them gets it, the other becomes enraged in jealousy because he wants to take what the other employee got, but can't.

Now, let's switch scenarios. The C.E.O. of a billion-dollar company wants to promote his favorite employee and give him a huge raise. But the employee refuses to take the raise. Now the boss is feeling a different type of jealousy. Do you see the difference?

God gets extremely jealous when He can't give us everything He has for us. He knows that intimacy with Him is better than

---

[126] See 1 Kings 18

anything and everything in this world. When we are entangled with the shallowness of this world, we cannot experience the fullness of His holy romance. This drives the Lord to jealousy.

> "You're cheating on God. If all you want is your own way, flirting with the world every chance you get, you end up enemies of God and his way. And do you suppose God doesn't care? The proverb has it that 'he's a fiercely jealous lover.' And what he gives in love is far better than anything else you'll find" (James 4:5 MSG).

The main thing we must learn about the jealousy of God is not how potentially heartbreaking we can be to Him, but how passionate He is about us.

In fact, the best defense against breaking His heart is understanding His fiery passion for us. Nothing changes us like the changeless love of Jesus.

How Much Do You Desire Him?

After His resurrection, Jesus went undercover. He showed up on the road to Emmaus and started conversing with two of His disciples. But they couldn't recognize Him because He somehow hid His glory from them. So these disciples started preaching to the Lord, about Jesus of Nazareth, and how He had just been crucified. (As if Jesus didn't know anything about that. It's a hilarious episode if you think about it.)

Then, the undercover Jesus started to give those two disciples the Bible study of all Bible studies, breaking down the Old Testament, and showing the oblivious disciples the deep truths of how the Scriptures point to Jesus Christ. I can just picture those two disciples salivating.

You Are His Bride

When the disciples got to their location, and it seemed that Jesus was going to just walk away. Luke records, "As they approached the village to which they were going, Jesus acted as if he were going farther" (Luke 24:28-29 NIV).

Wait a minute! Why would Jesus act like He was going to keep walking away from them? Jesus was testing them. He was wondering, "How much do they desire Me? Are they content without My presence? Are they OK with not having My voice? Now that they got to Emmaus, will they no longer want Me?"

By the way, Emmaus means "warm spring."[127] It speaks of a place of comfort. Unlike the early church that was plagued by persecution, in America many Christians and churches have reached the plateau of comfort. But, Jesus is asking the burning question, "Now that they are comfortable, do they still desire Me?"

"Is anyone among you suffering? Let him pray. Is anyone cheerful? Let him sing psalms" (James 5:13 NKJV).

The Scriptures tell us to pray when things are tough, but when things are good, we are to sing praises. Both prayer and praises are expressions of our desire for the Lord. In every season of our lives, we must desire Him.

The two disciples rightly refused to be content with Christ-less comfort, so they urged Jesus strongly. When they saw Jesus' bluff, the Scriptures record, "They urged him strongly, 'Stay with us, for it is nearly evening; the day is almost over.' So he went in to stay with them" (Luke 24:28-29 NIV).

---

[127] http://en.wikipedia.org/wiki/Emmaus

NEVER BURN OUT: Discover the Reality of your Identity

Our Bridegroom Wants to Be Wanted

A few years ago, I felt the Lord's presence drifting from my life and ministry. I started to wonder if He was upset with me. During this dry time I remember asking a minister to pray for me for my intimacy with God to be restored. I told her, "It's not like it used to be, I really miss Him." She told me, "What you are feeling is really His feelings for you. You are sensing how much He misses you, and you are interpreting it as your own feelings. You see, He misses intimacy with you more than you ever could."

Then I realized that the Lord wasn't mad at me, but rather madly in love with me, and He was just longing for me to urgently seek Him out.

Those two relentless disciples ended up having an unforgettable encounter with the Lord. Priceless encounters with Jesus belong to the lovesick Bride!

> "You will seek me and find me when you seek me with all your heart" (Jeremiah 29:13 NIV).

Are you a comfortable, lazy Christian? Or, are you a lovesick bride? "Lovesick" means you are so in love that you are unable to act normally.[128] As we come to know Jesus as our Bridegroom, our lives will be anything but normal, and the opposite of boring.

Desiring Jesus is the key to a pure heart. 1 John 3:2-3 tells us that those who long for Jesus' return are purifying themselves. Harmful bacteria cannot grow or remain when the heat goes up. That is why in many places people boil their water before they drink it. In the same way, the filth of this world cannot grow, or remain, in a heart that is burning for Jesus the Bridegroom. A pure heart is a burning heart. It's His fiery passion for us that causes our hearts to boil for Him.

---

[128] http://www.thefreedictionary.com/lovesick

Chapter 11

Honor Your Birthright

Myles was raised in a small two-bedroom house in the Bahamas.[129] His sisters slept in one room, his parents slept in the other room, and he and his brothers slept on the floor where bugs bit them and rats ran over them.

Due to his skin-color, he was treated as a second-class citizen. In middle school, one of his teachers told him, "You're retarded. You can't learn. You are just an advanced monkey."

Myles wept because he believed his teacher.

When Myles shared the teacher's comment with his mother, his mother assured him that it wasn't true. She commanded him to memorize Ephesians 3:20.

> "Now to him who is able to do far more abundantly than all that we ask or think, according to the power at work within us" (Ephesians 3:20 ESV).

---

[129] Story taken from Session 3, International Leadership Conference, Iglesias de Restauracion, May 28, 2011

As Myles repeated this verse over and over, it made his spirit leap with faith. He decided to honor God's Word above any other word.

Today, we know him as Dr. Myles Munroe.

In my opinion, He is one of the greatest Bible teachers and the most inspiring motivational speaker I've ever heard. He is a scholar of scholars who has written over forty books. He is a consultant to government officials and Fortune 500 companies; a true world-class leader. If he had honored the word of his teacher above the Word of God, he would not be where he is today.

Do you honor what God has to say about you? In other words, do you honor your birthright?

Birthright or Beans?

Esau came home famished from a hard day of work. Esau was a manly hunter, while his twin brother Jacob was a momma's boy. Due to his throbbing stomach, Esau asked his younger brother to cook him a meal.

But Jacob demanded Esau's birthright as the price. The story goes on to tell us that Esau acted like an idiot, and accepted this transaction. He traded his birthright for beans. Of course, this was very displeasing to the Lord.

The writer of Hebrews, writes, "That there be no immoral or godless person like Esau, who sold his own birthright for a single meal. For you know that even afterwards, when he desired to inherit the blessing, he was rejected, for he found no place for repentance, though he sought for it with tears" (Hebrews 12:16-17 NASB).

Jacob honored the birthright; Esau didn't. Do you honor your birthright? How you answer that question determines your

Honor Your Birthright

destiny. It determines if you will experience burn-out or ever-increasing revival.

What we've covered in the last ten chapters tells you about your birthright. Every true Christian has a heavenly birthright.

What is a birthright? According to Webster's Dictionary, a birthright is: "a right, privilege, or possession to which a person is entitled by birth."

When we were born-again, there were rights, privileges, and possessions that were given to us. Throughout this book we have covered truths about your birth-right:

1. Ever-increasing revival is your birthright.
2. Your birthright says you are a new creation.
3. Your birthright says you are righteous.
4. Your birthright says you are holy.
5. Dominion is your birthright.
6. Your birthright says you are in the new covenant of grace.
7. Your birthright says you are a walking revival.
8. Your birthright says you are adopted.
9. Your birthright says you are the Bride of Christ.

When we were born-again, there were rights, privileges, and possessions that were given to us.

Jacob ended up inheriting the following ten blessings because he honored the birthright.[130] If you honor your birthright,

---
[130] See Genesis 27:28-29

NEVER BURN OUT: Discover the Reality of your Identity

your identity in Christ, by grace, through the cross, then expect the following ten blessings to overtake you too.

10 Blessings for Those Who Honor Their Birthright

1) Jacob was promised **"the dew of heaven"** – This speaks of the glory! Honoring our new identity in Christ brings greater glory into our lives!

2) **"The fatness of the earth"** - This speaks of prosperity! Honoring our new identity in Christ brings prosperity, so we can have our needs met and be in the position to be able to give to others.

3) **"An abundance of grain"** – This speaks of the harvest of souls for us in the New Covenant. Honoring our birthright will empower our evangelism!

4) **"New wine"** – This speaks of joy in the Holy Spirit for us in the New Covenant! Those who believe in their identity in Christ will experience the joy of the Lord which is our strength!

5) **"Many people will serve you"** – This speaks of promotion! Those who honor the promises of God regarding their identity will experience supernatural favor and promotion like Joseph.

6) **"Nations will bow down to you"** – For us, this speaks of successfully making disciples of all nations, which is the Great Commission. Those who truly know their blood-bought identity will ask God for the nations, and will shake the nations for Jesus!

7) **"Be master of your brothers"** – This speaks of leadership! Those who understand who they are in Christ, what they

Honor Your Birthright

have in Christ, and what they can do in Christ, will have people looking up to them and following them.

8) **"Your mother's sons will bow to you"** – This speaks of honor! The men and women of God who I deeply honor are those who have strong faith in who they are in God.

9) **"Cursed be those who curse you"** – This speaks of divine protection!

10) **"Blessed be those who bless you"** – This speaks of being a channel of blessing! When we know who we are in Christ and who Christ is in us, we will be blessed to be a blessing to the world.

Our Father in heaven also wants to bless us with these ten blessings, but the big question is, "Do we honor our birthright?"

If we despise our birthright, we will miss out big time. That is why this book was written to help you to understand, appreciate, enjoy and honor your birthright. Now, for those who want to be careless about their birthright, what will be their lot in life? Carefully observe what Esau inherited, and see the parallels for Christians who devalue, underestimate, and are ignorant of their birthright.

7 Curses for Those Who Dishonor Their Birthright[131]

1) **"Away from the fertility of the earth shall be your dwelling"** – This speaks of the absence of prosperity.

2) **"Away from the dew of heaven from above"** – This speaks of the absence of the manifest presence of God. While Jacob honored the birthright and inherited ever-increasing revival, Esau didn't understand the value of his birthright and inherited an ever-decreasing revival!

---
[131] See Genesis 27:38-41

3) **"By the sword you shall live"** – This speaks of striving in human effort! Those who don't have faith in their In-Christ identity will not soar in the Spirit, but strive in their flesh.

4) **"Your brother you shall serve"** - This speaks of lacking leadership. An insecure Christian, who has no clue of how big God is in him or her, will not be the leader God's designed him or her to be.

5) **"You become restless"** – This speaks of fatigue. Many Christians burn out because they lack of revelation of who we are in Christ. It's tiring trying to be someone you don't believe you are. Those who don't believe that they are righteous, holy, walking revivals will get exhausted trying to continue walking in righteousness, holiness, and revival.

6) **"You will break his yoke from your neck"** – This speaks of rebellion. Those who don't know how blessed they are in Jesus Christ are insecure. Insecurity is the breeding ground for pride. Rebellion is a common expression of pride.

7) After Esau received the curses from his father, the Scriptures tell us that, **"Esau bore a grudge against Jacob because of the blessing with which his father had blessed him...Esau said to himself, "...I will kill my brother Jacob"** (Genesis 27:41 NASB).

Christians who despise their birthright will be bitter and jealous people. Why? They will see their brothers and sisters in Christ who walk in the revelation of their birthright living so much more blessed!

Because of low self-esteem, which is the by-product of despising the birthright, they have their doors wide open for the spirit of envy and murder.

Honor Your Birthright

Does this describe you? It doesn't have to. On the other hand, don't make the mistake of thinking everyone will love you when you are walking in ever-increasing glory. There will always be haters.

Historically, revivals and revivalists were always opposed most ferociously not by the sinners in the world but by Christian brothers who didn't have revelation about their birthright.

Conclusion

In light of what you have discovered in this book, why should you ever burn out? Why shouldn't you experience ever-increasing revival? Why shouldn't you be a dominion-taking revivalist?

Why shouldn't you go from glory to glory; faith to faith; love to love? Why should your relationship with God be suffering instead of thriving? Why shouldn't you be totally filled with the power and presence of the Holy Spirit right now?

Remember:

- **You are in Christ.** The B.C. you is dead!
- **You are who you are by grace.** Your identity is not based on your performance!
- **You have been given all the benefits of the finished work of the Cross!**
- **You are a new Creation.** You have God's DNA; you have God powers and God senses!
- **You are Righteous.** You have been forgiven and clothed in righteousness!

NEVER BURN OUT: Discover the Reality of your Identity

- **You are Holy.** You are not common, but extraordinarily sacred!
- **You are called for dominion.** You have what you need to be successful in life!
- **You are in covenant with God.** The Almighty God is your resource and has your back!
- **You are a Walking Revival.** There is so much power and glory on the inside of you!
- **Mr. Revival is living in you.** You are not His stop-over or time-share, but His home!
- **You are Adopted.** You have a loving Father who delights in you!
- **You are the Bride of Christ.** You are the focal point of His unquenchable passion!

So, there is no legitimate reason for you not to be totally overtaken by the power and love of God. It's yours. Take it in Jesus' name!

Addendum

How to Kill a Revival

They called him Prime Time.

He's the only man to have played in both the Super Bowl and the World Series. Deion Sanders is a rare athlete – who had the privilege of playing professional football and baseball. As a Hall-of-Famer, he sure knew the game of football. But when he switched from being in the National Football League to playing Major League Baseball, he had to change his mentality and switch his identity. If he had still believed that he was in the NFL and started taking the ball and running with it, he wouldn't have done too well! If he still saw himself as a football player, and tried to tackle the opponent who was running, he would have been heavily fined. And, if he refused to change, he would have killed his career.

Now, did you know that there are many Christians who are in the league of the New Covenant, but they still have an Old

NEVER BURN OUT: Discover the Reality of your Identity

Covenant mindset, and it has been keeping them from truly succeeding? In fact, it has been causing burn out and killing revivals.

So, what is the Old Covenant mindset? And, what is the New Covenant mindset? Please, keep reading.

I'm not down-playing the Old Covenant. We ought to read the Old Testament, because all Scripture is inspired by God and profitable to us.[132] The Old Covenant was holy and precious. But it was limited. Although the New Covenant and the Old Covenant do share some common themes and principles, the New Covenant is now a different ballgame, and we must recognize that.

Don't misunderstand – God doesn't change in the New Covenant; He's the unchanging God. But the coming of Jesus Christ and His history-altering work on the cross changed the game. It didn't change God's standards of holiness, but it changed our identity!

The Old Covenant with it's holy laws were given to reveal God's holiness and also our desperate need for a Savior.[133] Through the Old Covenant, we realize that we can't live right and be right on our own, apart from Jesus Christ. As we come to faith in Jesus, we are now in the New Covenant. Jesus said that John the Baptist was the greatest man in the Old Covenant, but the least in the Kingdom was greater than John.[134] Jesus was saying everybody in the New Covenant had received a greater identity than anyone in the Old Covenant. This is not a reason to brag; rather, it's greatly humbling. In the New Covenant, Christ does for us what we couldn't do for ourselves!

[132] See 2 Timothy 3:16
[133] See Galatians 3:24
[134] See John 7:28

Addendum: How to Kill a Revival

It's "a far better covenant with God, based on better promises" (Hebrews 8:6 NLT). The Old Covenant is the beautiful starry backdrop that makes the fireworks of the New Covenant more apparent.

How to Experience Ever-Fading Glory

"The old way [The Old Covenant], with laws etched in stone, led to death, though it began with such glory that the people of Israel could not bear to look at Moses' face. For his face shone with the glory of God, even though the brightness was already fading away. Shouldn't we expect far greater glory under the new way [The New Covenant], now that the Holy Spirit is giving life? "If the old way [The Old Covenant] which brings condemnation, was glorious, how much more glorious is the new way [The New Covenant] which makes us right with God! In fact, that first glory was not glorious at all compared with the overwhelming glory of the new way. So if the old way, which has been replaced, was glorious, how much more glorious is the new, which remains forever! ...And we [New Covenant people], who with unveiled faces all reflect the Lord's glory, are being transformed into his [Jesus'] likeness with ever-increasing glory, which comes from the Lord, who is the Spirit" (2 Corinthians. 3:7-11 NLT & 18 NIV – inserts are mine).

There are a two simple truths that I hope you caught from the passage above. First, there was glory in the Old Covenant, but it was a fading, diminishing glory. Second, in the New Covenant, we have an overwhelming, ever-increasing glory – a greater glory!

NEVER BURN OUT: Discover the Reality of your Identity

One day, as I was reading this passage, the Holy Spirit began showing me that the Old Covenant mentality will actually cause glory to fade from our experience, while the New Covenant mentality is a real key to ever-increasing glory!

The Holy Spirit continued to show me that Moses had great glory on his face – but it was not an ever-increasing glory. It was actually an ever-fading one. Then, He revealed to me that those with an Old Covenant mindset can technically experience the powerful glory of God, but sadly, it will eventually diminish right out of their experience.

Defining the Old Covenant

When I refer to the Old Covenant, I'm referring to the period of time that covers the the period from Exodus 19 to the death of the Lord Jesus – also known as the Law of Moses. However, the Old Covenant era is out of date.[135] Jesus fulfilled it;[136] and He opened up the New Covenant to us through His death on the cross.[137]

When Jesus cried from the cross, "It is finished!" (John 19:30), it was the Greek term "tetelestai." This is one Greek term worth studying. Greek scholar Rick Renner explained this profound Greek word, writing, "In classic Greek times, the word tetelestai depicted a turning point when one period ended and another new period begun. The Cross was 'the Great Divide' in human history. When Jesus cried out, 'It is finished!' He was shouting that the Old Covenant had ended and the New Covenant had begun."[138]

Is it possible to be living in a New Covenant era – but still have an Old Covenant mindset?

---

[135] See Hebrews 8:13
[136] See Matthew 5:17
[137] See Luke 22:20, Hebrews 9:16-17
[138] Rick Renner, *Paid in Full*, p. 208

Addendum: How to Kill a Revival

Sadly, yes.

Andrew Murray, the South African author, wrote that, "Many Christians still walk in Old Covenant bondage."

Therefore, Paul urged his readers to "be transformed by the renewing of the mind" (Romans 12:2 NASB). If you have an Old Covenant mindset, you have not renewed your mind. Paul beckoned the believers in Jesus to study the Word of God so we are "rightly dividing the word of truth." (2 Timothy 2:15). If you have an Old Covenant mindset, you are failing to rightly divide the word of God.

The un-renewed mind cannot sustain the ever-increasing revival! When we underestimate the power of the cross, which divides the Old Covenant from the New, we cannot sustain ever-increasing revival.

As we saw at the beginning of this book, New Covenant believers already have the potential for going from glory to glory resident within them, but embracing an Old Covenant mindset will paralyze that potential.

So, what is the Old Covenant mindset? And what is the New Covenant mindset? Please, keep reading.

Old Wineskins Can't Hold New Wine

Remember when Jesus said, "No one pours new wine into old wineskins. If he does, the wine will burst the skins, and both the wine and the wineskins will be ruined. No, he pours new wine into new wineskins"? (Mark 2:22 NIV).

What was Jesus talking about here?

Old wineskins are already stretched to the max, and therefore, when new wine enters the old wineskin, you will soon lose both the wine and the skin, because the nature of the new wine is to expand. It's worth noting that old wineskin can temporarily hold new wine, but because of the ever-increasing nature of the new wine, soon the old wine-skin will pop, and the new wine will be lost.

The old wineskins represent the Old Covenant mindset. Old wineskins can only temporarily carry new wine – which is the ever-increasing revival we've been talking about.

The Old Covenant mentality will not be able to contain the ever-increasing glory of the New Covenant! So, if you have an Old Covenant mindset, you technically can experience God's New Covenant glory; you can get saved in revival, experience the glory of God, and even enjoy revival for a few years, but eventually it will spill out of your experience! Sadly, this has happened throughout Church history to many historic revivals, to many churches, to many ministers and to many Christians.

The Old Covenant vs. the New Covenant

In the book of Galatians, the Apostle Paul refers to Ishmael as a picture of the Old Covenant, and Isaac as a picture of the New Covenant.[139] Which Covenant was God's perfect will?

Ishmael was not God's perfect will for Abraham,[140] Isaac was. Likewise, the Old Covenant was not and is not God's perfect will for His people, while the New Covenant is. It wasn't God's perfect will that the blood of bulls and goats would make His people righteous, but that the blood of Jesus Christ would

---

[139] See Galatians 4:22-31
[140] Remember, Ishmael was born as the result of Abraham and Sarah growing impatient and slipping out of the will of God by deciding that Abraham would procreate with their slave-woman Hagar.

Addendum: How to Kill a Revival

ultimately accomplish that task! The Word states that "It is impossible for the blood of bulls and goats to take away sins ... we have been sanctified through the offering of the body of Jesus Christ once for all" (Hebrews 10:4 & 10 ESV).

After comparing the two covenants, Paul makes it clear that we who have received the New Covenant need to expel the Old Covenant ways of thinking just like Sarah expelled Ishmael after Isaac was born. "But what does the Scripture say? 'Get rid of the slave woman and her son, for the slave woman's son will never share in the inheritance with the free woman's son'" (Galatians 4:30 ESV).

In the eyes of God, the Old Covenant system was flawed; [141]not because His holy laws were imperfect, but His people were, and they were not capable of becoming righteous and born-again through their performance.[142] God, in His perfect judgment, knew that the Old Covenant needed to be replaced by the New Covenant. So, He sent His prophets, Jeremiah and Ezekiel, to prophesy the coming of the New Covenant.[143] And then He ultimately sent His only begotten Son to shed His precious blood to give us the New Covenant.

If the Old Covenant was good enough for God, why would He have sent His own Son to the cross?

A dominating characteristic of the Old Covenant was the law of Moses, while the dominating characteristics of the New Covenant are the grace and truth that came through Jesus.

"For the law was given through Moses; grace and truth came through Jesus Christ" (John 1:17 ESV).

---
[141] See Galatians 4:22-31
[142] See Romans 3:20
[143] See Jeremiah 31:31-33, Ezekiel 11:19, 36:26

NEVER BURN OUT: Discover the Reality of your Identity

Moses was the Mediator of the Old Covenant, while Jesus is the Mediator for the New. Those in the Old Covenant stumbled into finding their identity in their law-keeping; that's the Old Covenant mindset, the old wineskin. However, we in the New Covenant find our identity in God's grace and truth, which is equivalent to finding our identity in Christ. That's the New Covenant mindset, the new wineskin.

Insulting or Exalting Jesus

An unthinkable price was paid for the New Covenant to be in effect, and therefore to stubbornly hold to an Old Covenant mindset, is an insult to Jesus Christ — who is the mediator of the New Covenant.

While Old Covenant mentality is insulting to Jesus, the New Covenant mindset is exalting of Him. And that is why the Apostle Paul wrote with the harshest tone in his letter to the church in Galatia. Under the total influence of the Holy Spirit, Paul unleashed on the Galatians saying, "You foolish Galatians! Who has bewitched you?" (Galatians 3:1 NIV). The Galatians were New Covenant believers who were falling back into the Old Covenant mentality. They were finding their identity in their law-keeping performance, rather than in the cross of Jesus and the grace of God.

You see, before the Galatians were duped, they were doing awesome. They were trusting in God's grace, finding their identity in Christ and enjoying ever-increasing revival as the result. However, when the false teachers started poisoning their minds, the Galatians started finding their identity in their flesh, by their works, and through their performance. Whenever we do this, we will be satanically set up for a burnout.

Addendum: How to Kill a Revival

Obviously, there is nothing wrong with keeping the commandments of God, but there is something wrong if we are finding our identity in our religious duties rather than in Christ.

Paul had just explained to the Philippians that he was perfect when it came to keeping all the external, meticulous rules of the Old Covenant.[144] He ran the race harder and faster than anybody, but then he wrote:

> "Indeed, I count everything as loss because of the surpassing worth of knowing Christ Jesus my Lord. For his sake I have suffered the loss of all things and count them as rubbish, in order that I may gain Christ" (Philippians 3:8 ESV).

It's not that Paul was against the Old Covenant laws, but he was against finding his identity in his law-keeping performance, rather than in Christ.

Moses was the Mediator of the Old Covenant, while Jesus is the Mediator for the New. While those in the Old Covenant, stumbled into finding their identity in the law-keeping, we in the New Covenant must find our identity in God's grace and truth, which is equivalent to finding our identity in Christ.

Spiritual Adultery

Paul spoke of the Old Covenant Law as being the ex-husband.[145] Those under the Old Covenant were married to the Law, and they were bound to Mr. Law by covenant.

What kind of husband was Mr. Law?

---

[144] As an ex-Pharisee, Paul only kept the external rules of the Old Covenant. He couldn't keep up with all the internal rules- such as, "Thou shall not covet." He might have kept the commandments of God externally, but not internally. Nobody can apart from Christ and the Holy Spirit.
[145] See Romans 7:1-6

He was a husband that demanded perfection, but wouldn't budge to help you with it, and he would condemn you for your shortcomings. In fact, he had "a ministry of condemnation"[146] and he was never wrong. Nobody was allowed to divorce him, and he couldn't die. In a marriage like that, imagine what the wife's self-image would be like.

How then, would those under the Old Covenant get free from the tyranny of Mr. Law? It's only through faith in Jesus Christ! Those who receive Jesus as Savior and Lord partake in His death and are, thereby, officially dead to a performance-based, legalistic lifestyle.

> "Therefore, my brethren, you also were made to die to the Law through the body of Christ, so that you might be joined to another, to Him who was raised from the dead, in order that we might bear fruit for God" (Romans 7:4 NASB).

What kind of husband is Jesus?

He is an affirming husband, who still calls us to a holy life, but sent the Holy Spirit to enable us to live holy.[147] Therefore, as those married to Jesus, our lives can be even more glorifying to God than those under the Old Covenant.

Who wouldn't want to be married to a husband like that?

> Jesus called out to all those living under the bondage of the Old Covenant system – which was made drastically more grace-less and legalistic by the Pharisees – and said, "Are you tired? Worn out? Burned out on religion? Come to Me. Get away with Me and you'll recover your life. I'll show you how to take a real rest. Walk with

---
[146] See 2 Corinthians 3:9.
[147] See Romans 7:6

Addendum: How to Kill a Revival

Me and work with Me – watch how I do it. Learn the unforced rhythms of grace. I won't lay anything heavy or ill-fitting on you. Keep company with Me and you'll learn to live freely and lightly" (Matthew 11:28 MSG).

Imagine how happy the spouse of Mr. Jesus would be. Good news – you are married to Him forever!

Why would anybody want to cheat on Mr. Jesus with Mr. Law? Mr. Law speaks condemnation over you, but Mr. Jesus speaks righteousness over you. Living with self-condemnation will burn you out, while understanding the gift of righteousness and His humbling grace fans the flames of ever-increasing revival.

A wife's self-identity was heavily wrapped up in who her husband was. Where do you find your self-identity? If we find our identity in our law-keeping performance, rather than in Christ, we are committing spiritual adultery.

Let's not forget that Mr. Law continues to teach us many important, timeless lessons; however, we define ourselves by Mr. Jesus. While we continually learn of God's holiness from Mr. Law, we continually find our worth and identity in Mr. Jesus.

Let's remember that New Covenant never promotes lawless living – which wants to throw God's holy standards out the window in the name of "freedom in Christ." That kind of thinking is sinful.[148]

The New Covenant promotes freedom from the legalism which says, "You are who you are because of what you've done for God." On the contrary, New Covenant grace says, "You are who you are because of what He's done for you in Christ."

---

[148] See 1 John 3:4

A Better Covenant with Better Promises

The New Covenant mentality – which is key to sustaining ever-increasing revival, is finding our identity in Christ, by grace, and through the cross. The New Covenant is a better covenant, because it's based on better promises.[149]

Here are some of the better promises that we have covered in this book:

While the Old Covenant commands you to "Try harder and change your life!", the New Covenant declares over you, "You have been changed into a New Creation in Christ." (Ch. 3)

While the Old Covenant calls you "transgressor!", the New Covenant tells you that you are "righteous" in Christ. (Ch. 4)

While the Old Covenant calls you "sinner!", the New Covenant tells you that you are "holy" in Christ. (Ch. 5)

While the Old Covenant declares, "You are under the power of sin and death", the New Covenant declares, "You have dominion to reign in life through Christ." (Ch. 6)

While the Old Covenant declares, "You are a covenant breaker!", the New Covenant declares, "I (Jesus) will never leave you or forsake you." (Ch. 7)

While the Old Covenant tells you that you need to "beg God to send revival and convince Him it's a good idea!", New Covenant declares, "You are a walking revival." (Ch. 8)

While the Old Covenant declares, "You are children of wrath", the New Covenant tells you that you are "chosen" and "adopted" in Christ. (Ch. 9)

---
[149] See Hebrews 8:6

Addendum: How to Kill a Revival

While the Old Covenant says, "You are a shameful adulterer", the New Covenant declares, "You are the glorious bride of Christ." (Ch. 10)

Old Covenant Law Was a Signpost Shouting, "You Need Jesus!"

As you can see, the Old Covenant helps people to see that they desperately need Christ. "Therefore the Law has become our tutor to lead us to Christ, so that we may be justified by faith" (Galatians 3:24 NASB). When people come to Christ, they receive a New Covenant identity. This doesn't mean that we don't need to study the timeless principles from the Old Covenant,[150] but it does mean that we find our identity in Christ, by grace, and through the cross.

> "For no one can ever be made right with God by doing what the law commands. The law simply shows us how sinful we are" (Romans 3:20 NLT).

Contrary to popular first century thought, the Old Covenant Law was never given so that people would try to work their way into salvation through their perfect track-record. That's like trying to swim across the Pacific Ocean with a broken arm. The Pharisees foolishly attempted this impossible task, and were filled with pride, because they thought they were a couple of feet further down than the mainline sinners.

The Law was given to humble a person, so that he or she would be in position to receive the New Covenant grace of our Lord Jesus Christ. The Law made us come to see that we were sinners in desperate need of a Savior because of our weak flesh, sinful deeds, and miserable failures.

---

[150] See 1 Timothy 1:8, Acts 7:53, Acts 7:38, Matthew 5:17-18, Romans 7:12, Psalm 19, and Psalm 119

"The Law came in so that the transgression would increase" (Romans 5:20 NASB).

Praise God, that we have now come to saving faith in Jesus Christ! Therefore, we must no longer see ourselves through Old Covenant lenses. But it is when the New Covenant Christian still defines himself by his weak flesh, sinful deeds, and miserable failures that he will burn out and will eventually kill his revival.

This is not to say we don't take ownership of our mistakes and repent of them, but I am saying that we must find our identity in Christ, by grace, and through the cross. We must take responsibility to confess and turn from the sins that we commit, but we must always trust what God's Word has to say about our true identity.

To simply sum up this chapter, nobody in the Old Covenant could say, "My true identity is who I am in Christ, by grace, and through the cross!" But you can. If you don't want fading glory or a diminishing revival in your life, you must.

To be fair to the Old Covenant, there was a measure of grace in the Old Covenant in that the Old Covenant had types and shadows (foreshadows) of Christ and the cross, but we in the New Covenant have the reality of the person of Jesus and the fulfillment of the finished work on the cross. Point being: those under the Old Covenant didn't have what you and I have! Thus, let's cherish what we have.

We have New Covenant lenses to see ourselves through.

Let's use them!

For Further Study:
NeverBurnOutBook.com

If you would like to contact the author or order more books, please write: PastorDHP@gmail.com

Additional copies of this book and other book titles from XP Publishing are also available at the "store" at XPmedia.com and bookstores.

BULK ORDERS: We have bulk/wholesale prices for stores and ministries. Please contact usaresource@xpmedia.com and the resource manager will help you. For Canadian Bulk Orders please email resource@xpmedia.com.

www.XPpublishing.com